AF597291

PASSED REMAINS

WILLIAMSBURG/GREENPOINT 1987–2007

ANDERS GOLDFARB

DCV

Design: Cara Galowitz

Essay: Bonnie Yochelson

Copy Editing: Howard Gotfryd

Image Editing: Max-Color, Berlin

Production Management: DCV

Printing and Binding:
Optimal Media GmbH

Front Cover:
West Street, Greenpoint, 2006
(detail)

Back Cover:
Lorimer Street (through window),
Greenpoint, 1999

Distribution and marketing: DCV
sales@dcv-books.com

ISBN: 978-3-96912-040-8
Printed in Germany

Published by

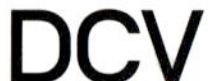

www.dcv-books.com

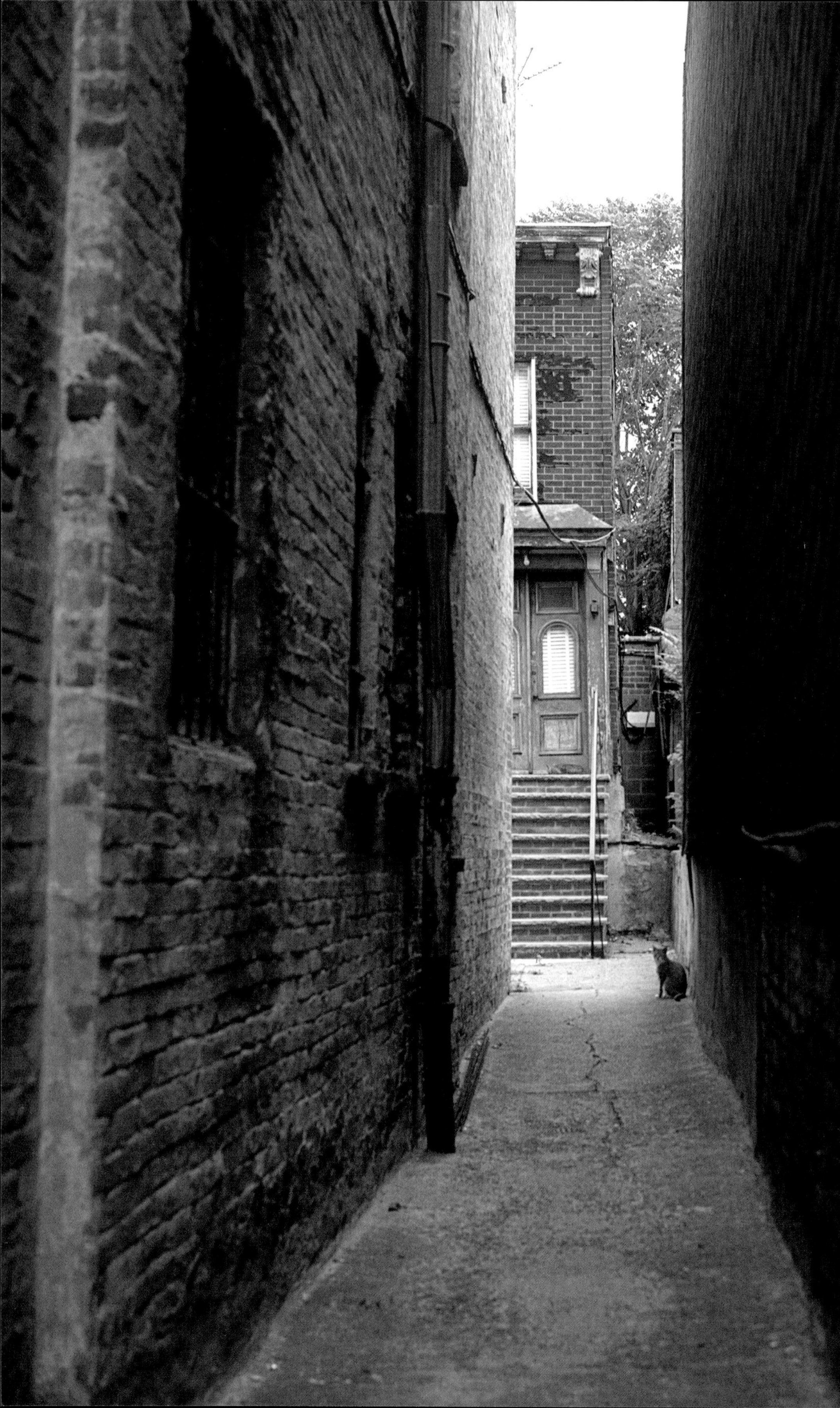

PASSED REMAINS BONNIE YOCHELSON

In 1986, when Anders Goldfarb moved to Greenpoint, Brooklyn, he joined a growing number of artists seeking the low rents of what was then a declining neighborhood of light industrial buildings and working-class residences. He soon began photographing in Greenpoint and neighboring Williamsburg, riding his bike around the area looking for the peculiar beauty of vinyl siding, peeling paint, and razor wire. Using filters to reveal the cumulus clouds on beautiful sunny days, he brought a sense of clarity and order to photographs of abandoned gas stations and burned-out buildings. The project ended twenty years later, as gentrification conquered the streetscape.

Following in the footsteps of Eugene Atget and Berenice Abbott, photography's great urban documentarians, Goldfarb has created a valuable record of a moment of transformation. His subject is not movement — there are few people in these photographs — but change, as seen in the effects of time on architecture.

Goldfarb was born in Crown Heights, Brooklyn, in 1954. His parents, Julius and Helen, were Polish Holocaust survivors who married in 1949 and had two children, Shelley and Anders. When he was a toddler, the family moved to Flushing, Queens, where they were the only Jews among Roman Catholics of Irish, German, and Italian descent. Although drawn to the artistic kids in high school, Goldfarb did not find photography until college at SUNY Stony Brook, where he took a darkroom course. The road to a career in photography was circuitous: on a post-college cross-country trip, Goldfarb stopped in Ann Arbor, where he enrolled in a BFA program at Eastern Michigan University before earning an MFA in photography at SUNY New Paltz, in 1986, at the age of 31.

Eschewing the cutthroat world of freelance photography, Goldfarb supported himself with teaching photography and printing for the Associated Press. He lived simply with his cat, photography books and equipment, and a three-speed Raleigh bicycle. After ten years with the Associated Press, he took

(Left): Driggs Avenue, Williamsburg, 2000

an unpaid leave of absence to devote himself to the Greenpoint project, biking around with a medium format Rolleiflex camera and many rolls of film in his backpack. A darkroom master, Goldfarb remains loyal to film, which, like the Rollei itself, is a relic of twentieth-century photographic practice.

The simplicity and modesty of Goldfarb's outdated tools extend to his subject, the remains of industrial, working-class Brooklyn. In a 2012 interview, Goldfarb professed that the scarred and abandoned structures he so lovingly photographed serve as metaphors for his parents, who were so deeply wounded by the war in Europe and remained unseen in America: "I photograph buildings that are outcasts… the pariah, the communist, the homosexual, the Jew, the gypsy…slated for demolition." Embarrassed by his rhetorical flourish, Goldfarb chuckled and added, "I never said that."

The interview ended with Goldfarb explaining that he always left one negative in his camera "because you never know," a phrase his father often said as a reminder of life's precarity. Perhaps unwittingly, Goldfarb has turned his father's pessimism on its head. Retaining the last negative suggests that you never know when an opportunity will present itself. Opportunities presented themselves often. *Passed Remains* offers a trenchant critique of American society and an affirmation of the creative spirit.

Bonnie Yochelson is an art historian and independent curator who specializes in photography of New York City. She has organized exhibitions and written books on Berenice Abbott, Alfred Stieglitz, and Jacob Riis, among others. For thirty years she taught in the MFA Photography and Related Media Program at the School of Visual Arts.

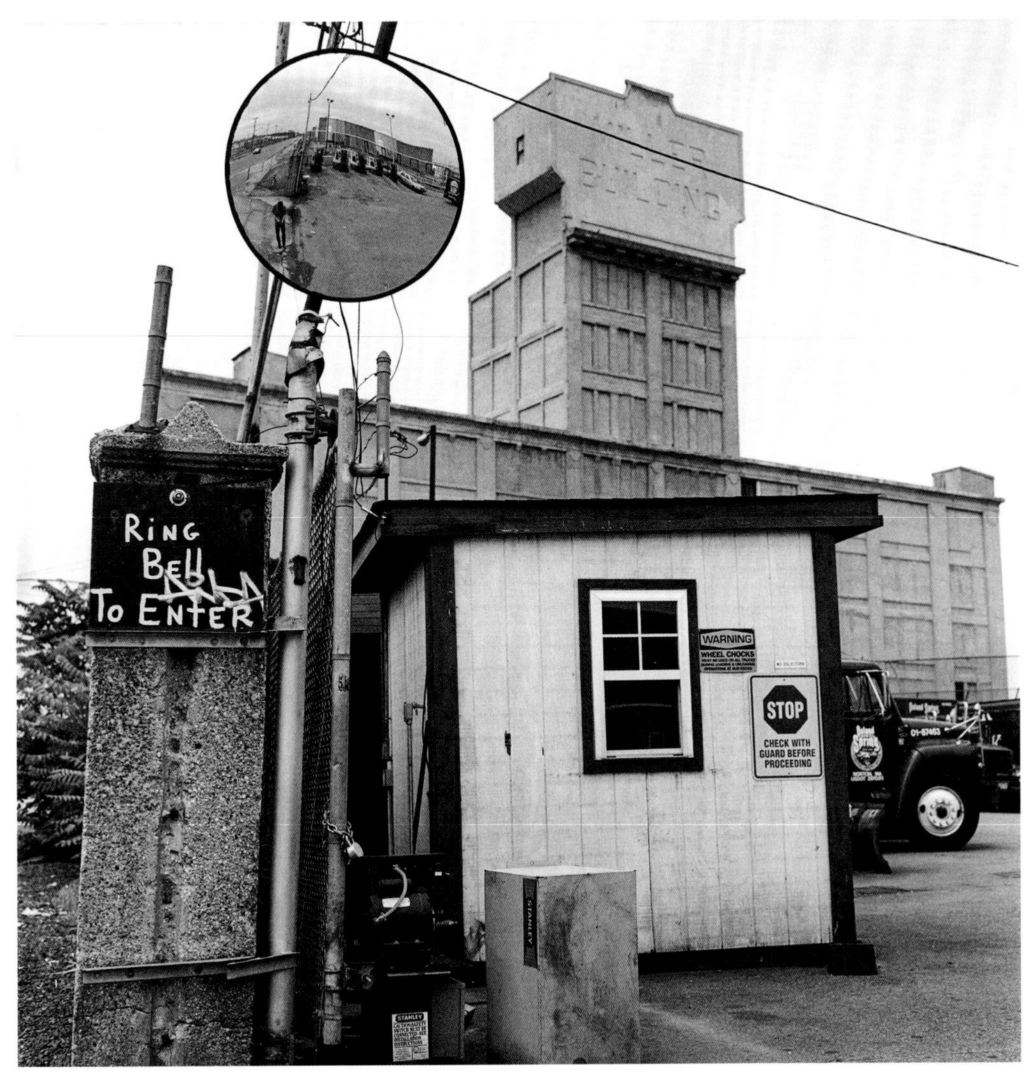
BUILDING
Ring Bell To Enter
WARNING
WHEEL CHOCKS
STOP
CHECK WITH GUARD BEFORE PROCEEDING
STANLEY

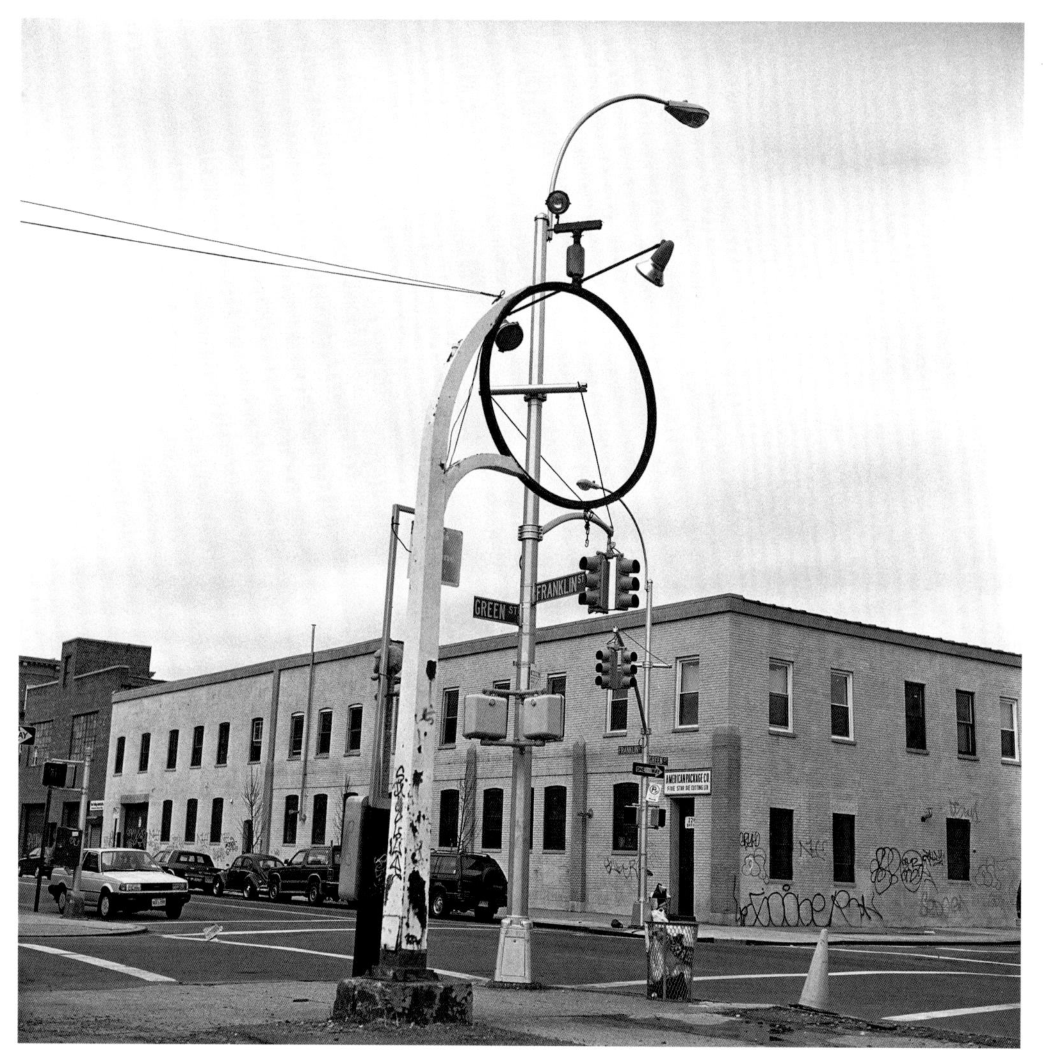
FRANKLIN ST
GREEN ST
ONE WAY
AMERICAN PACKAGE CO
FIVE STAR DIE CUTTING CO

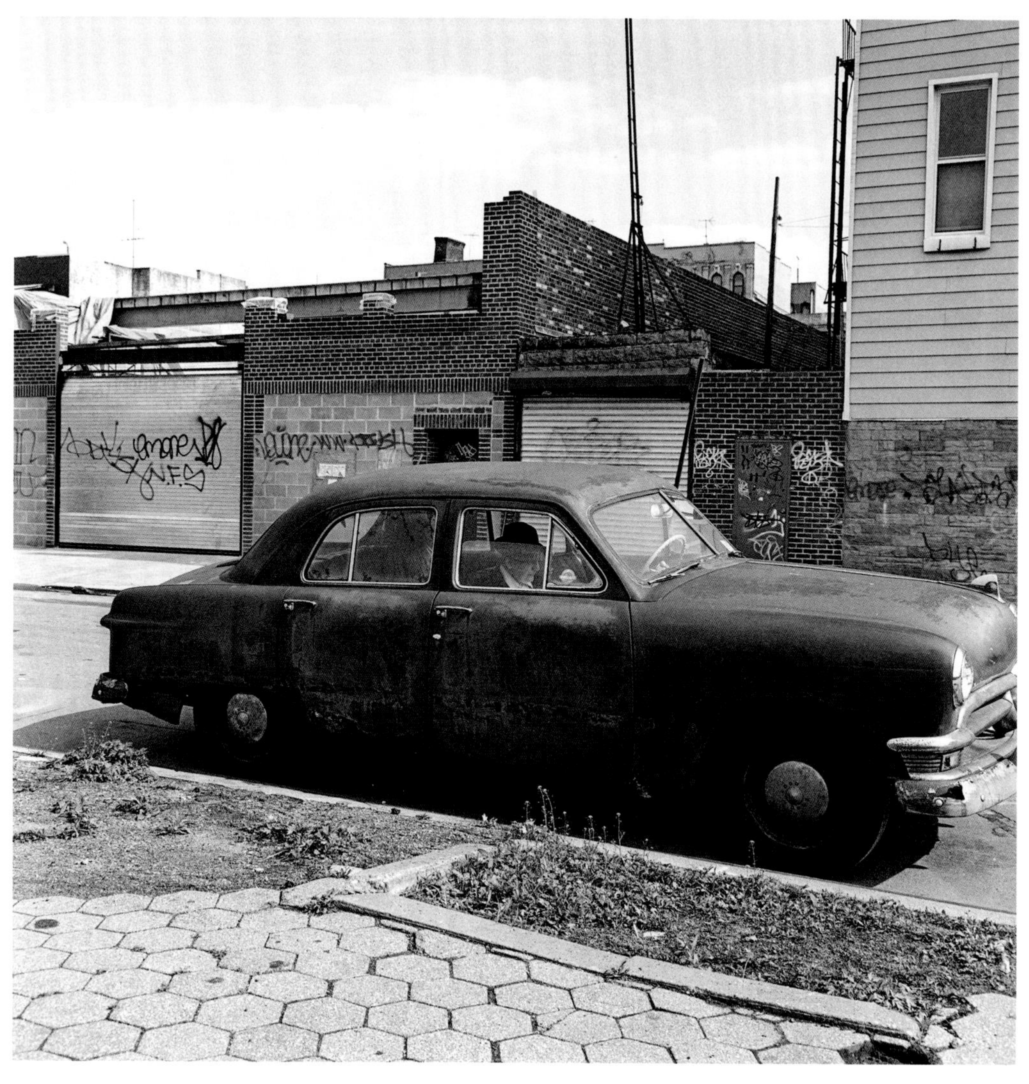

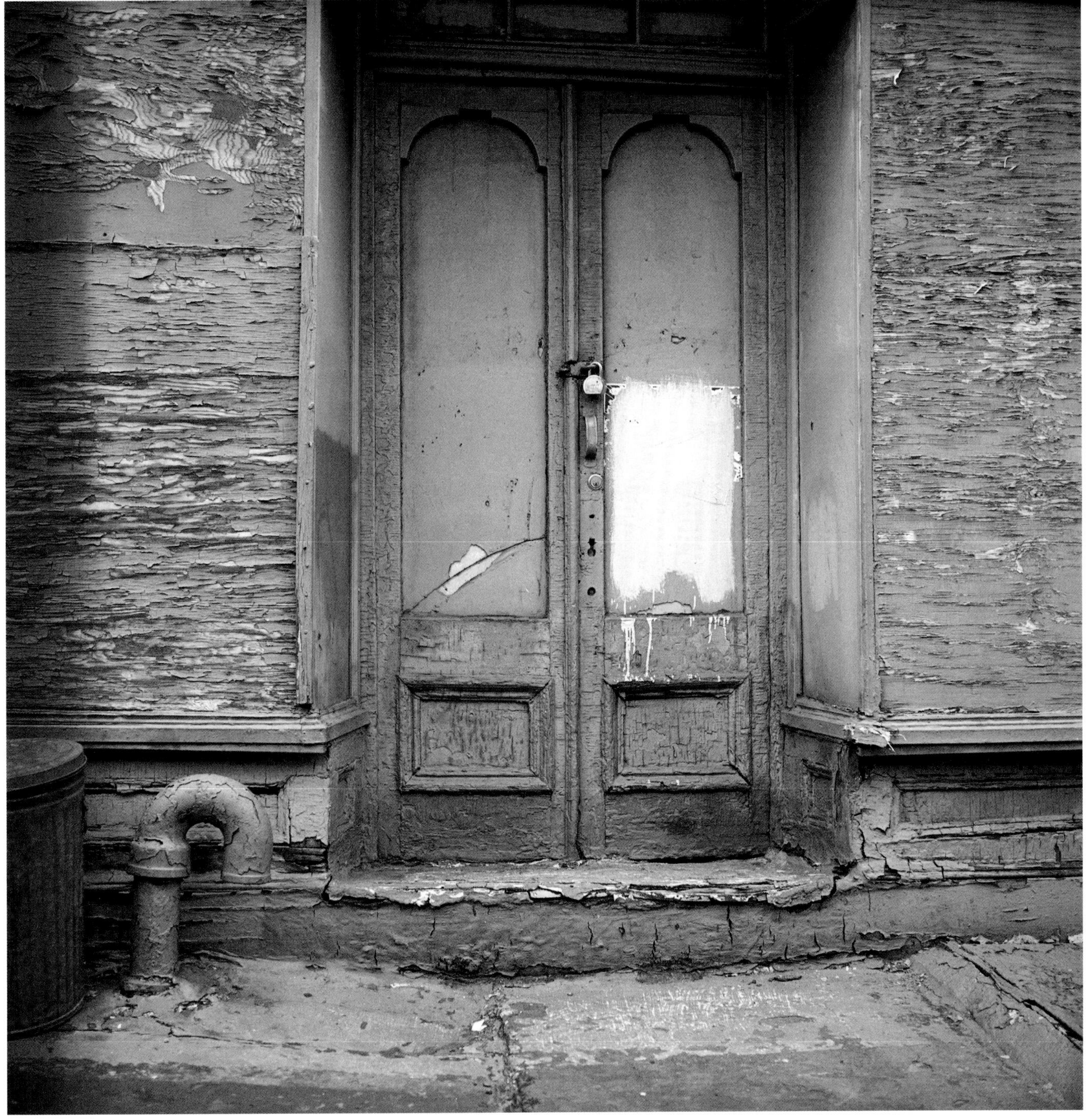

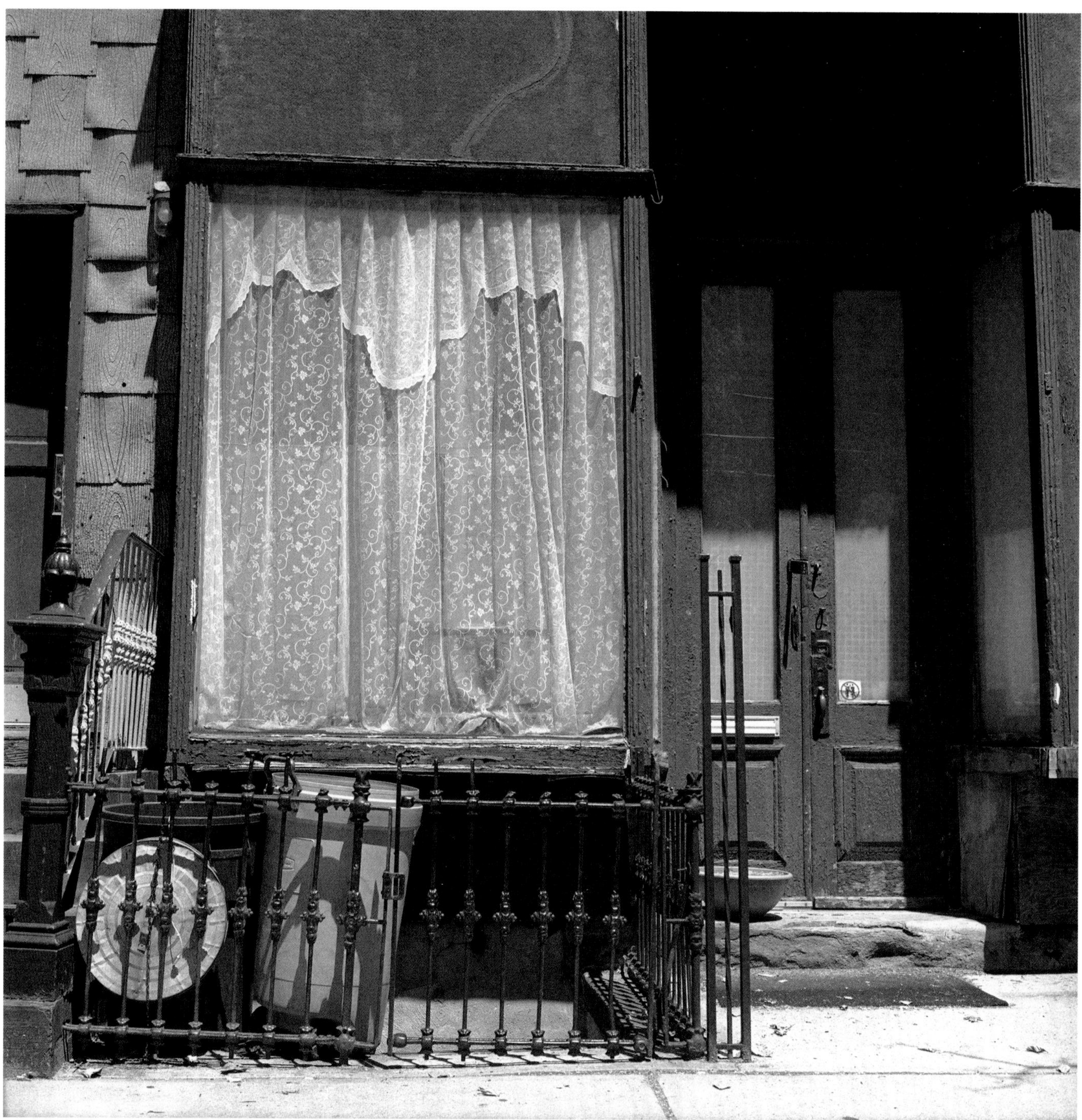

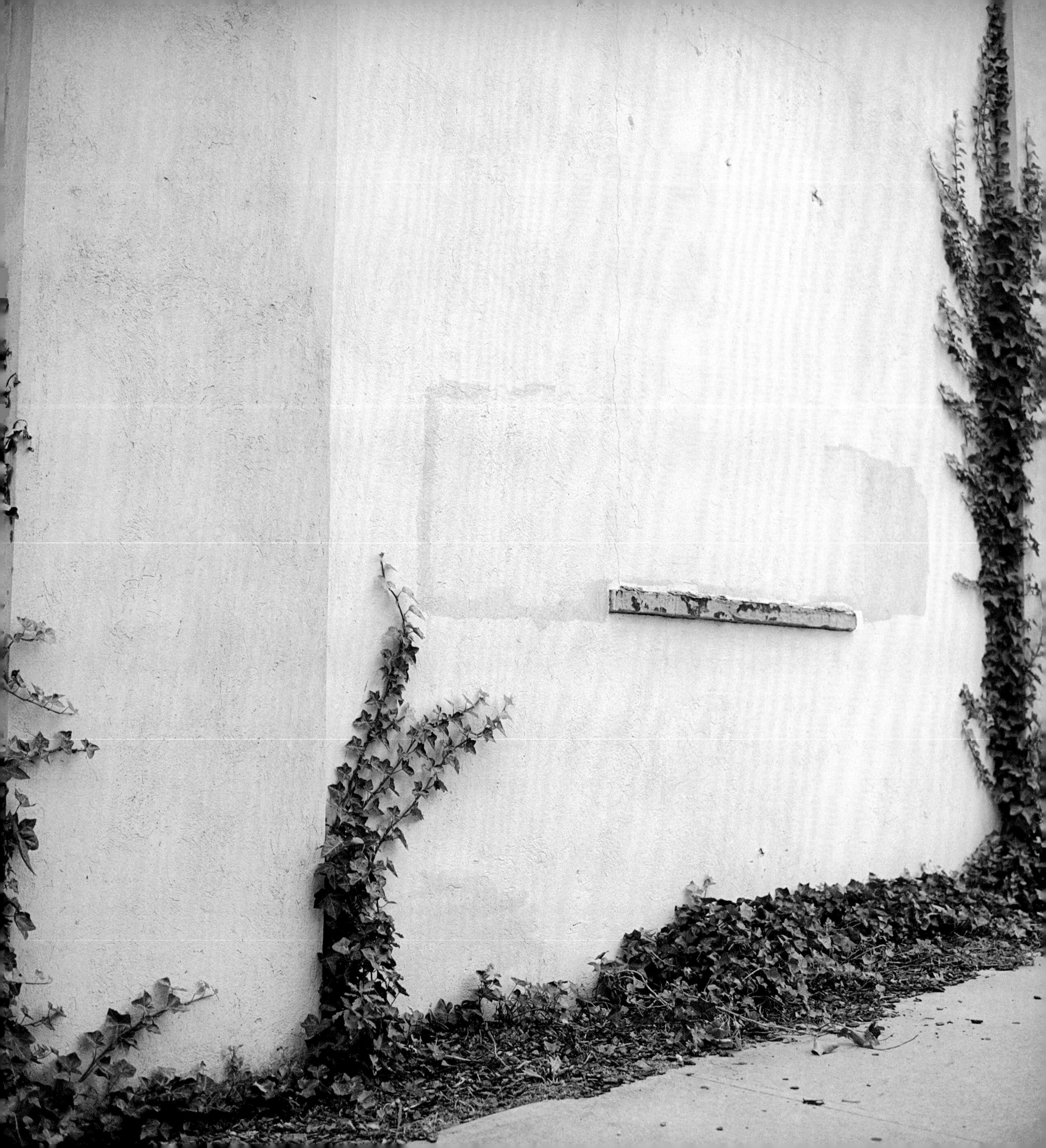

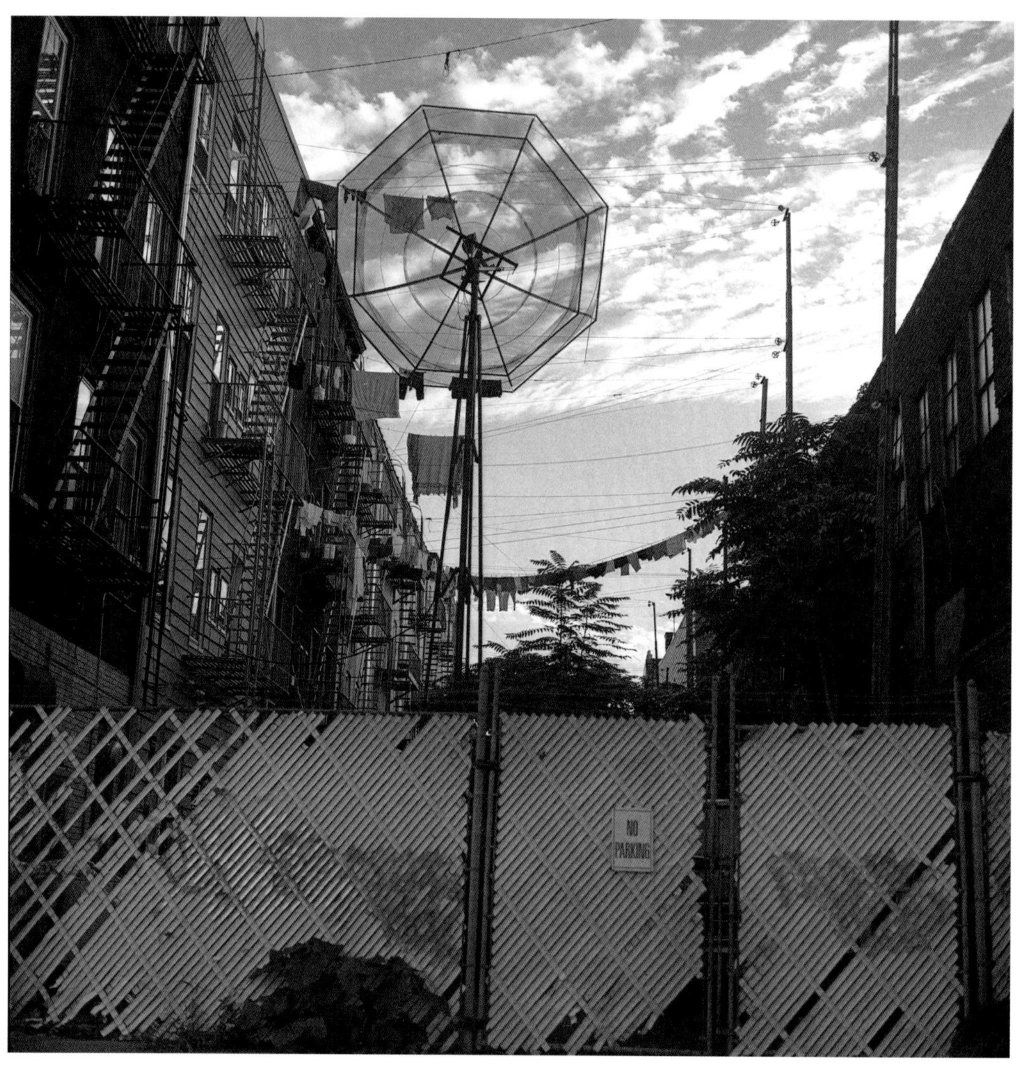
NO
PARKING

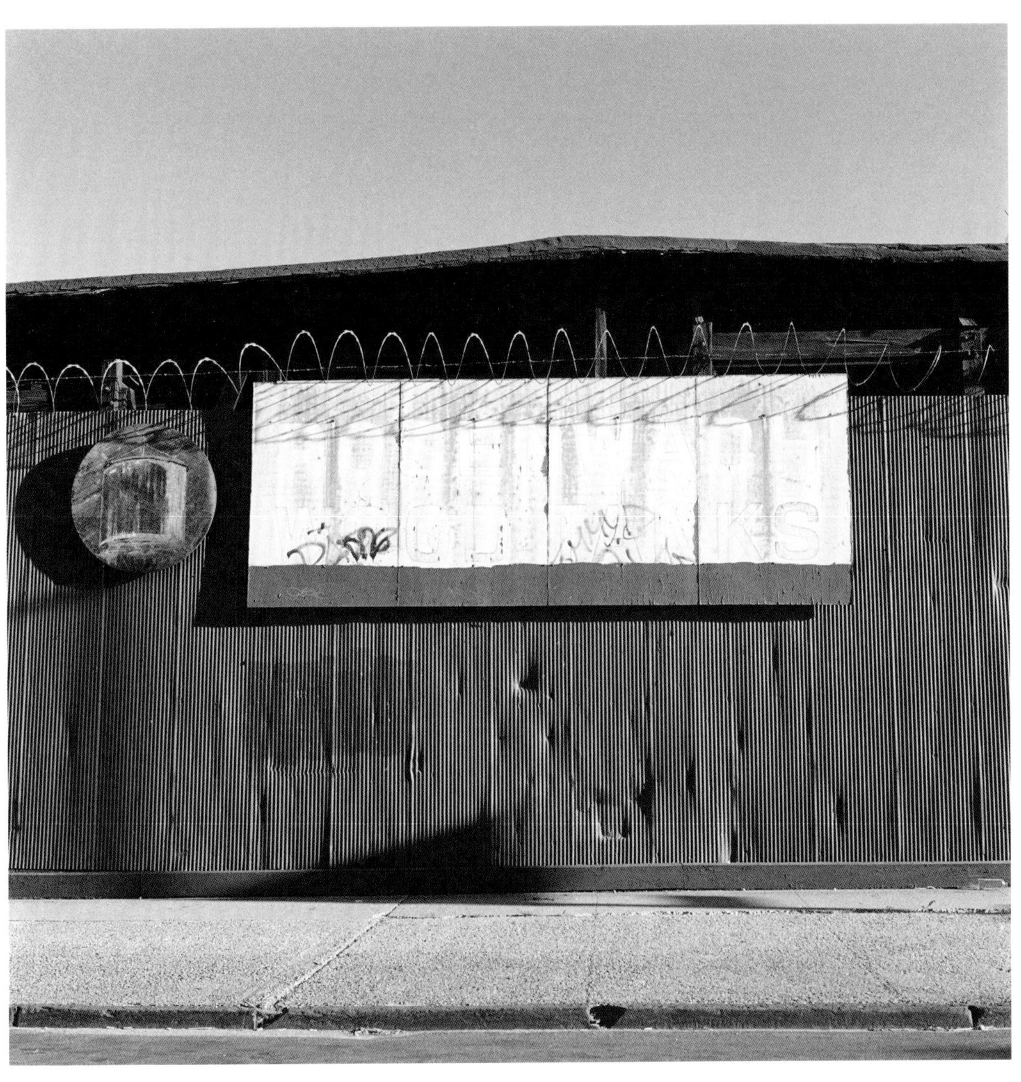

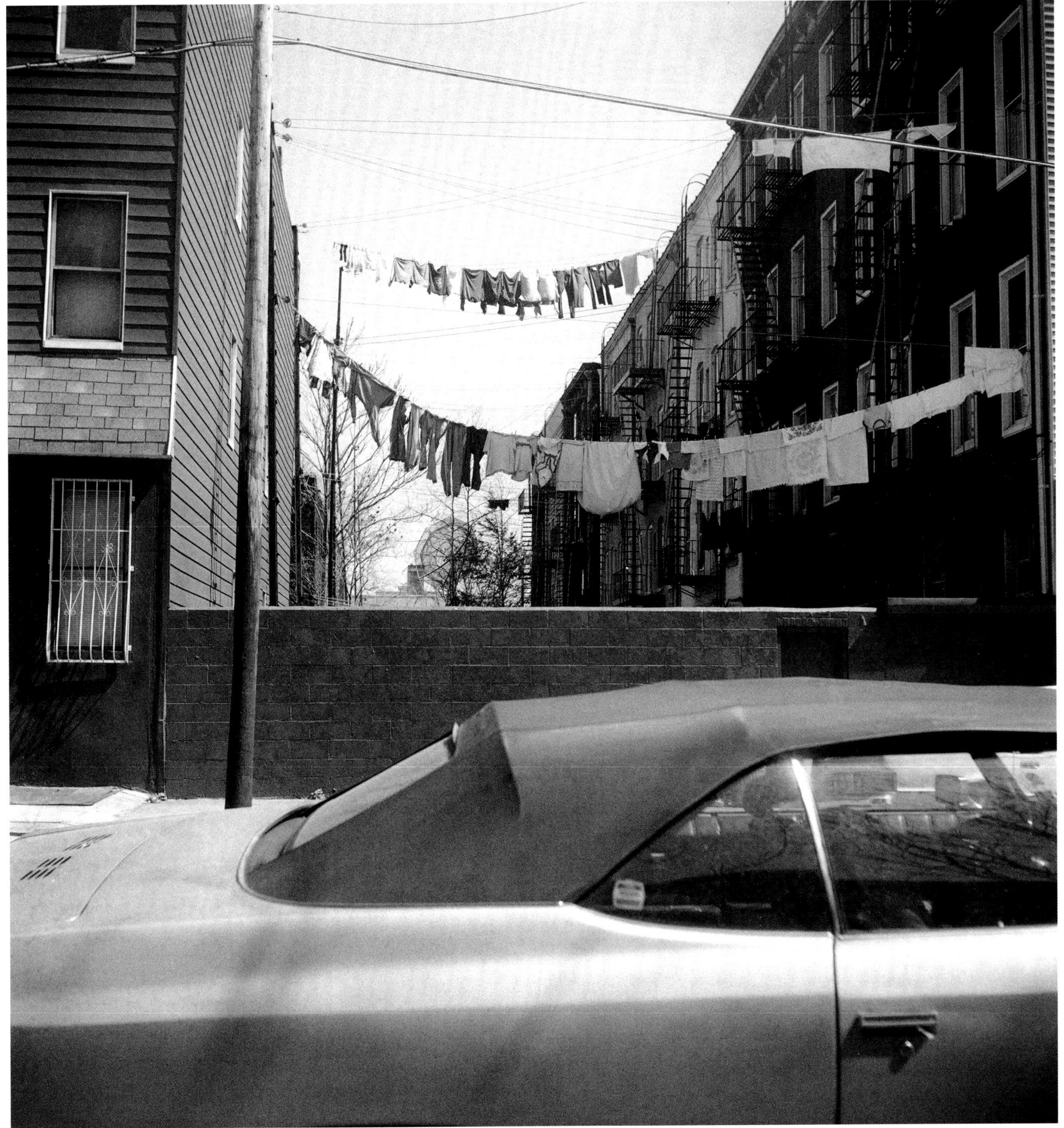

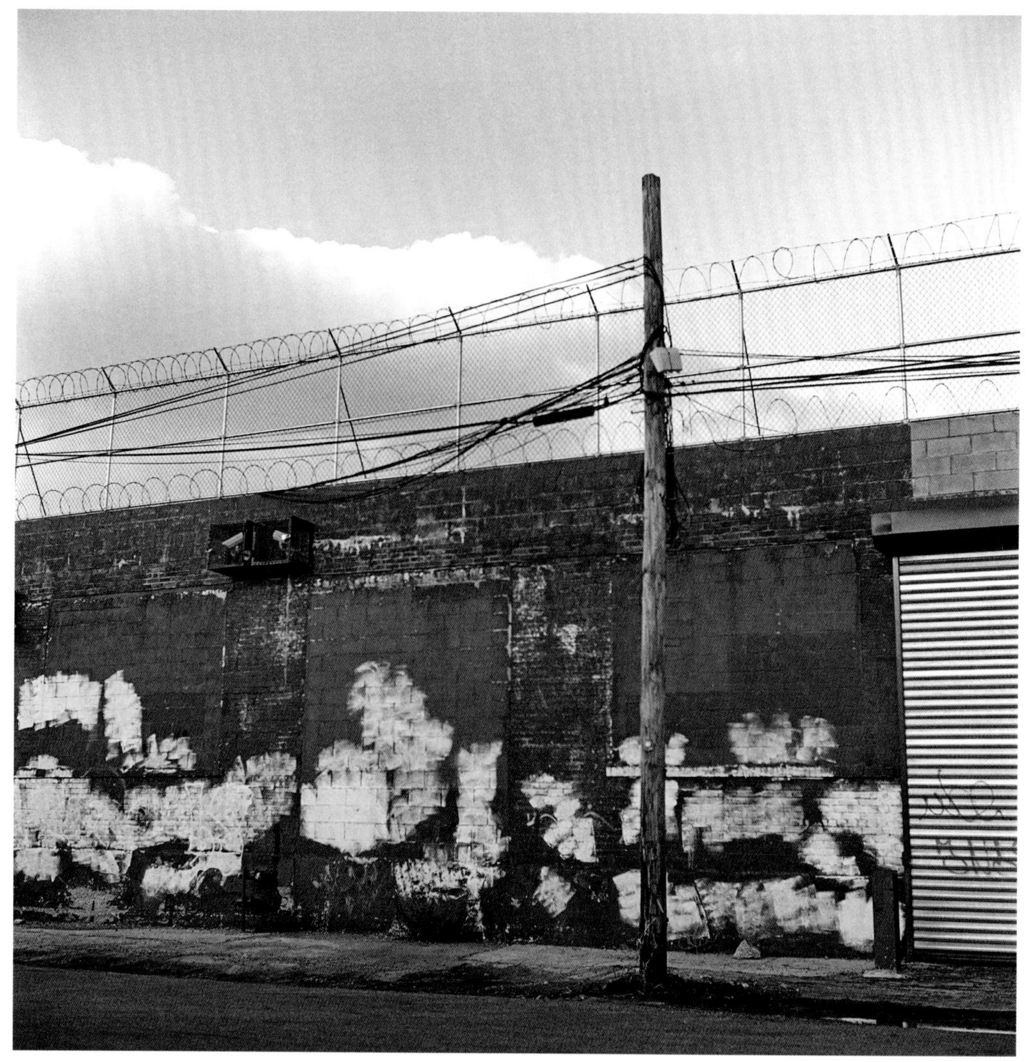

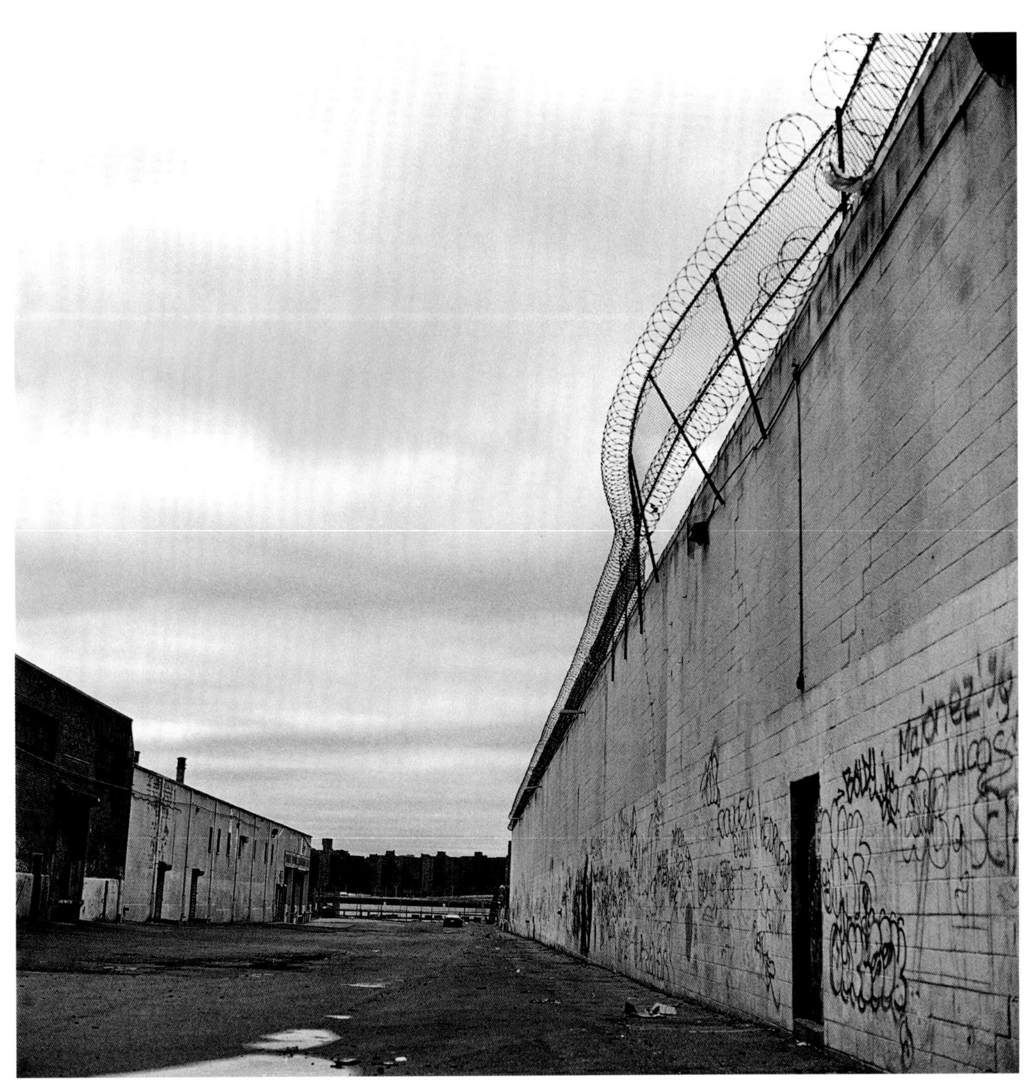

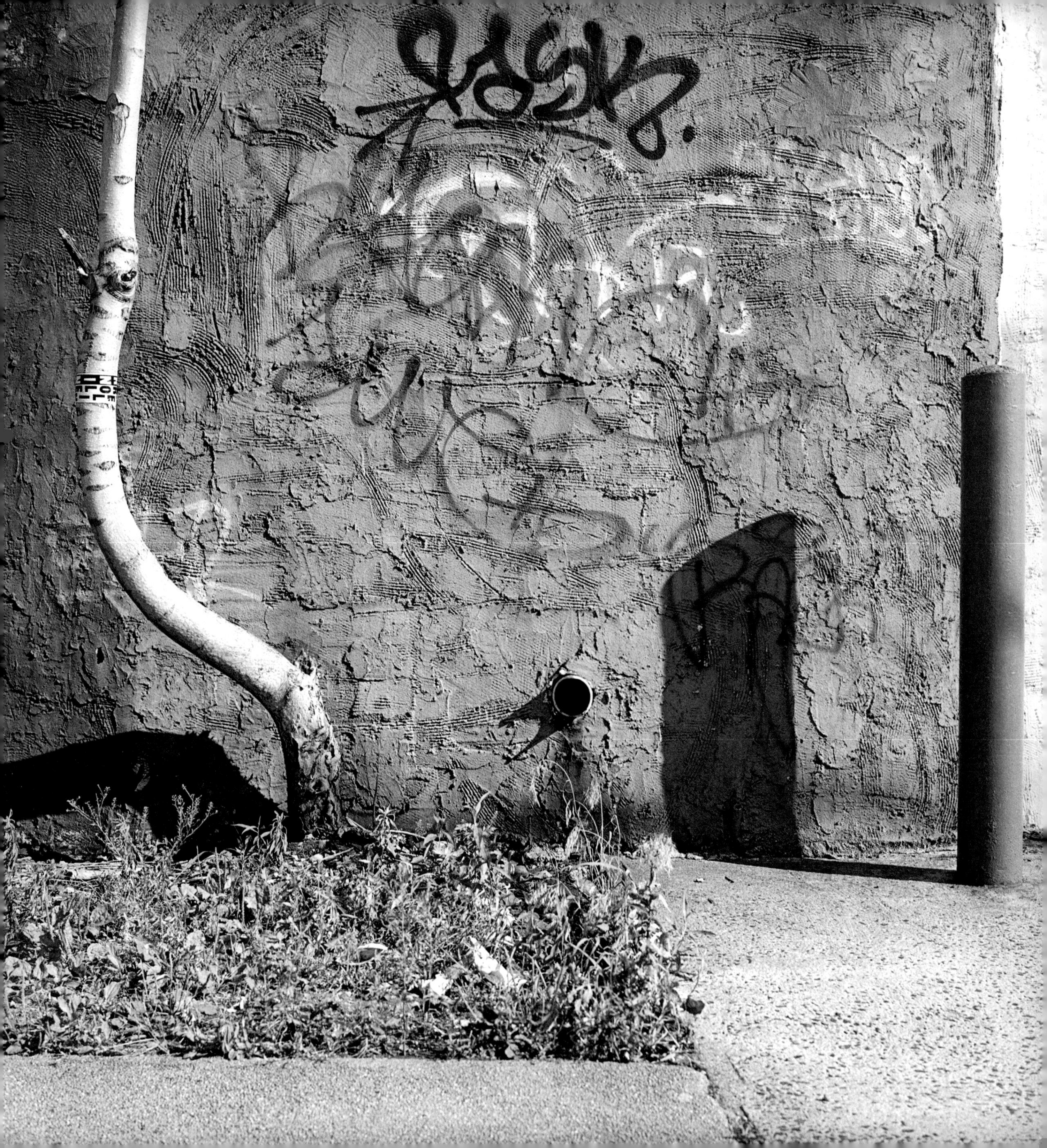

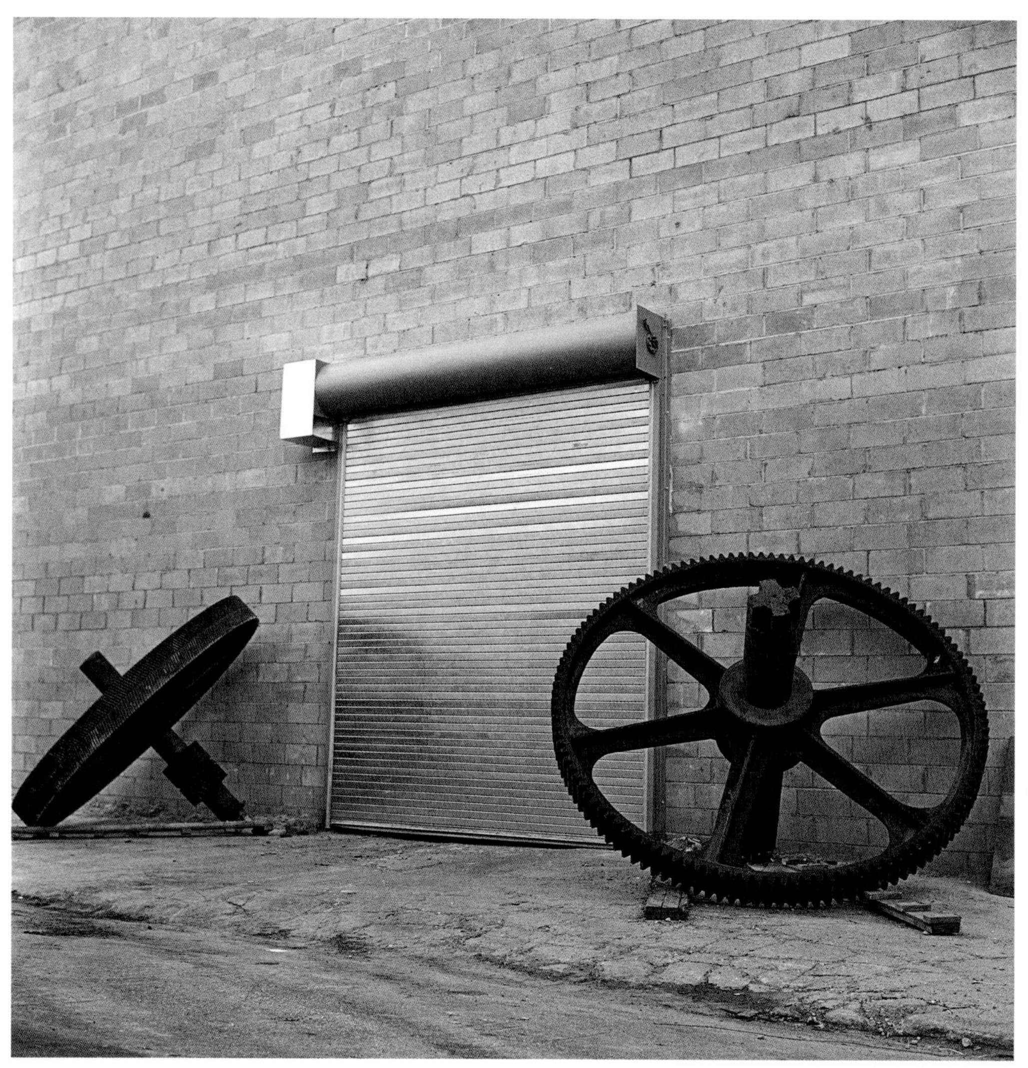

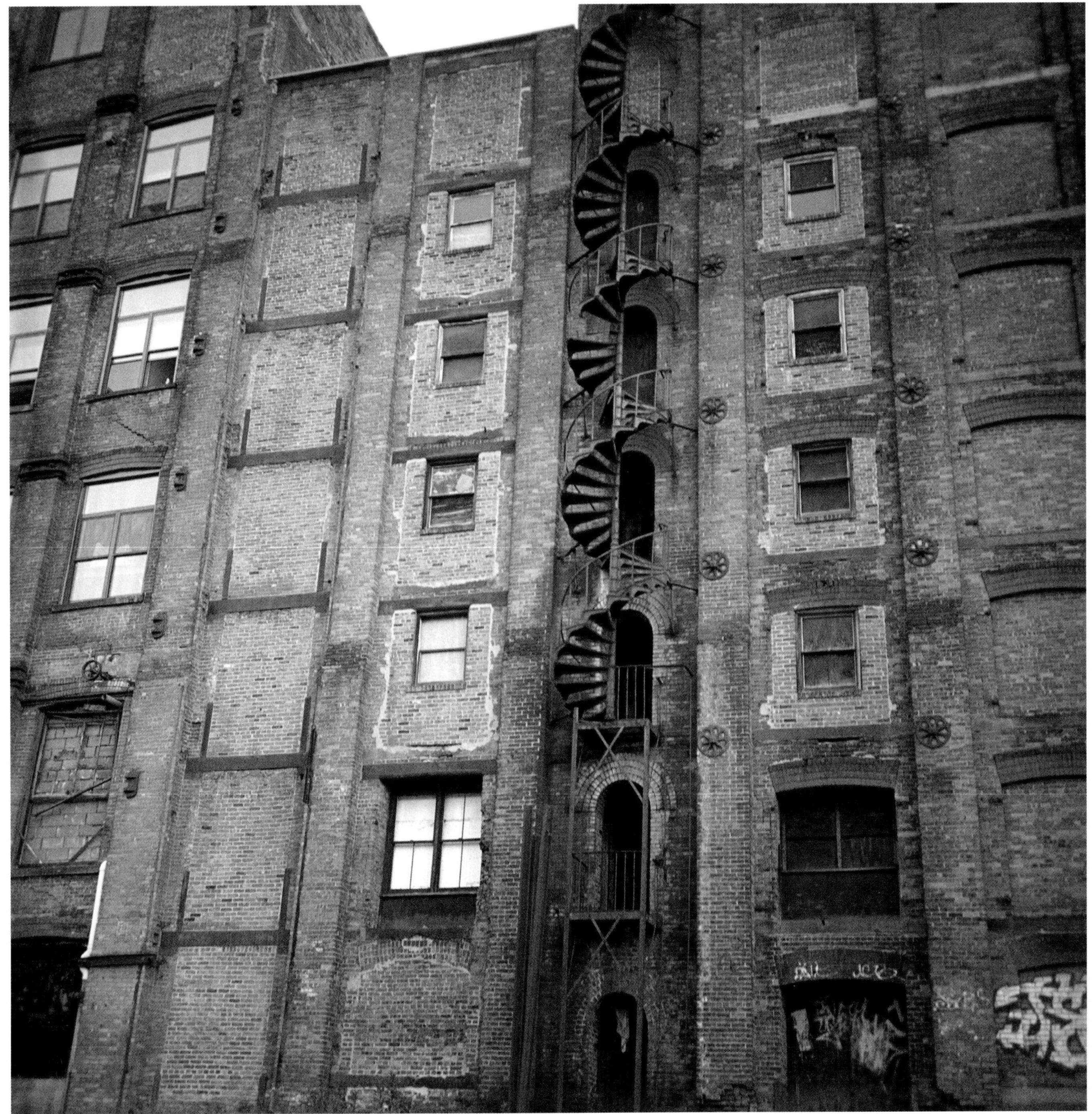

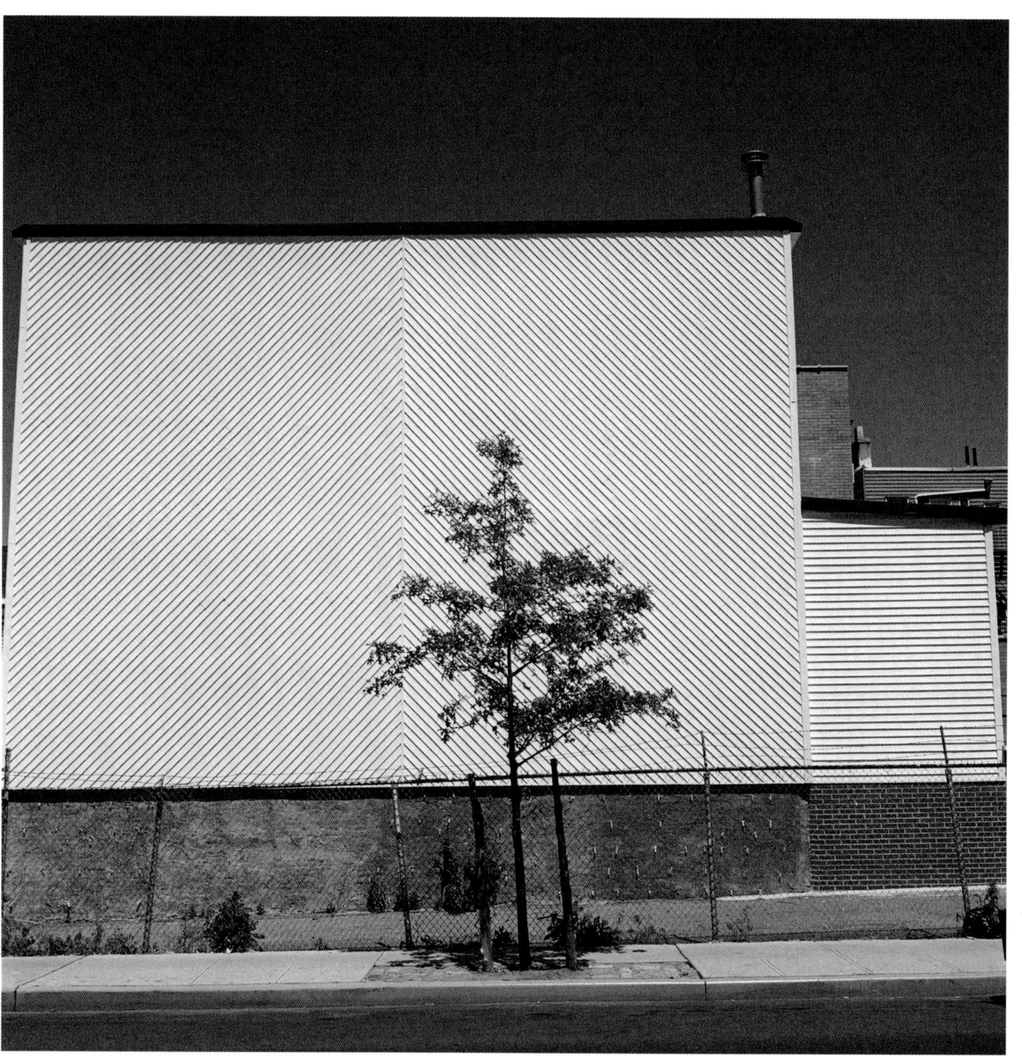

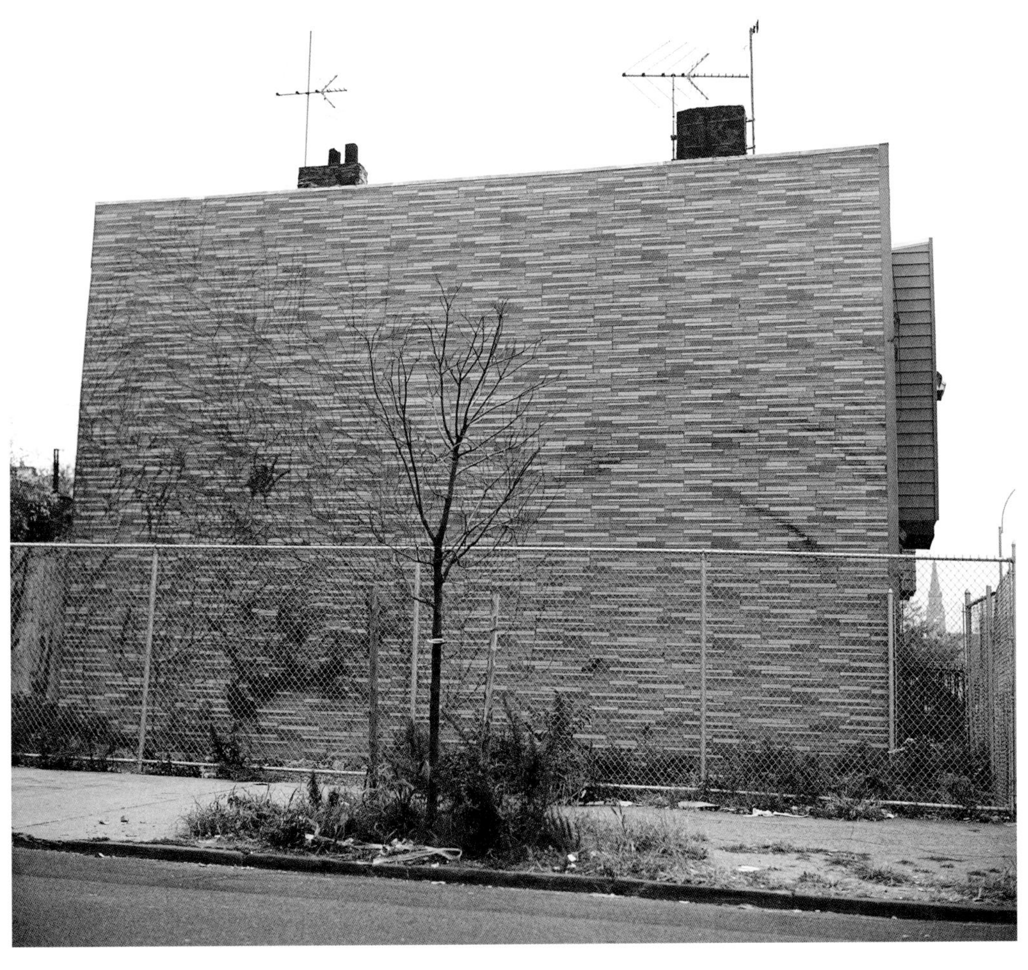

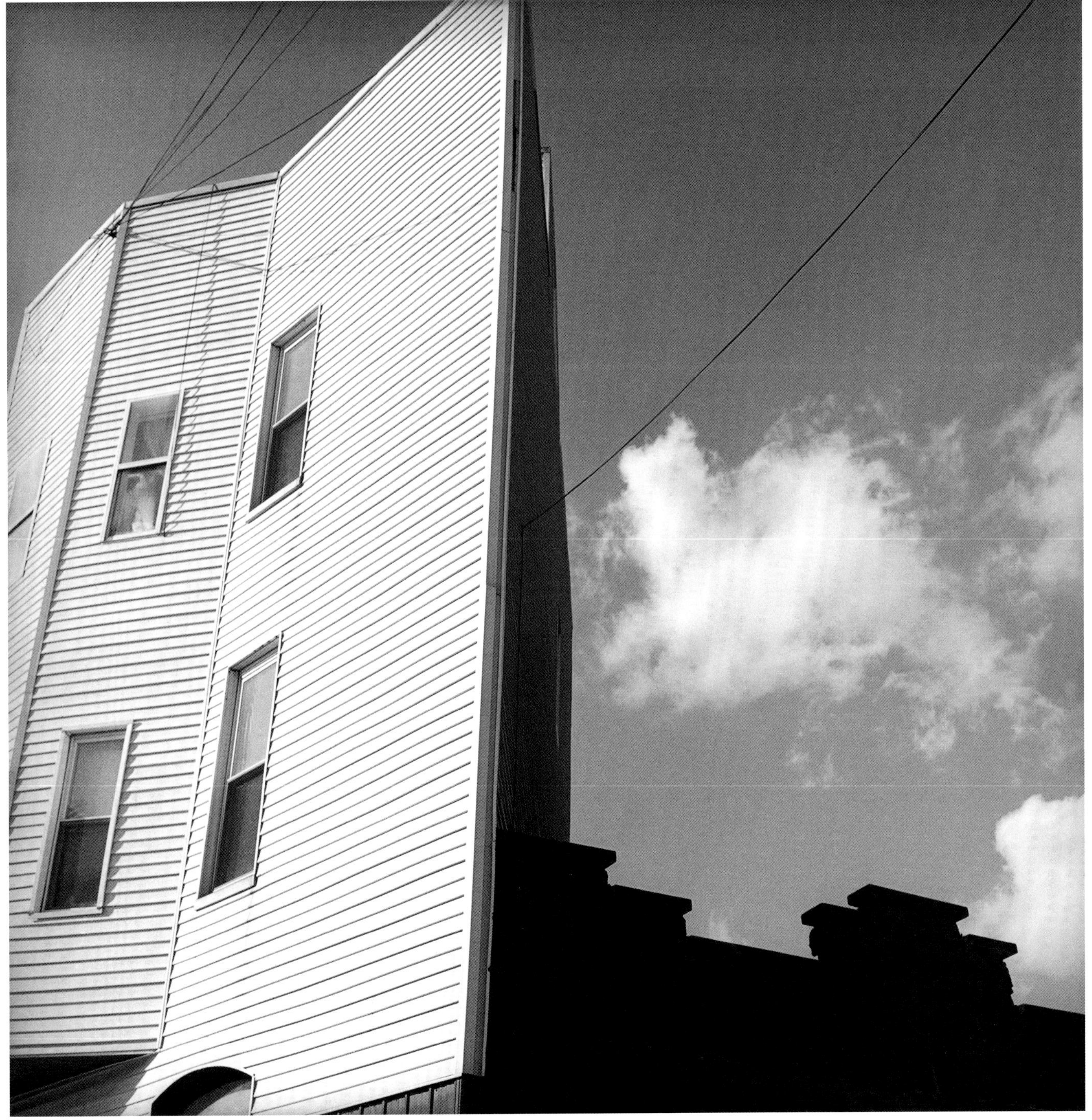

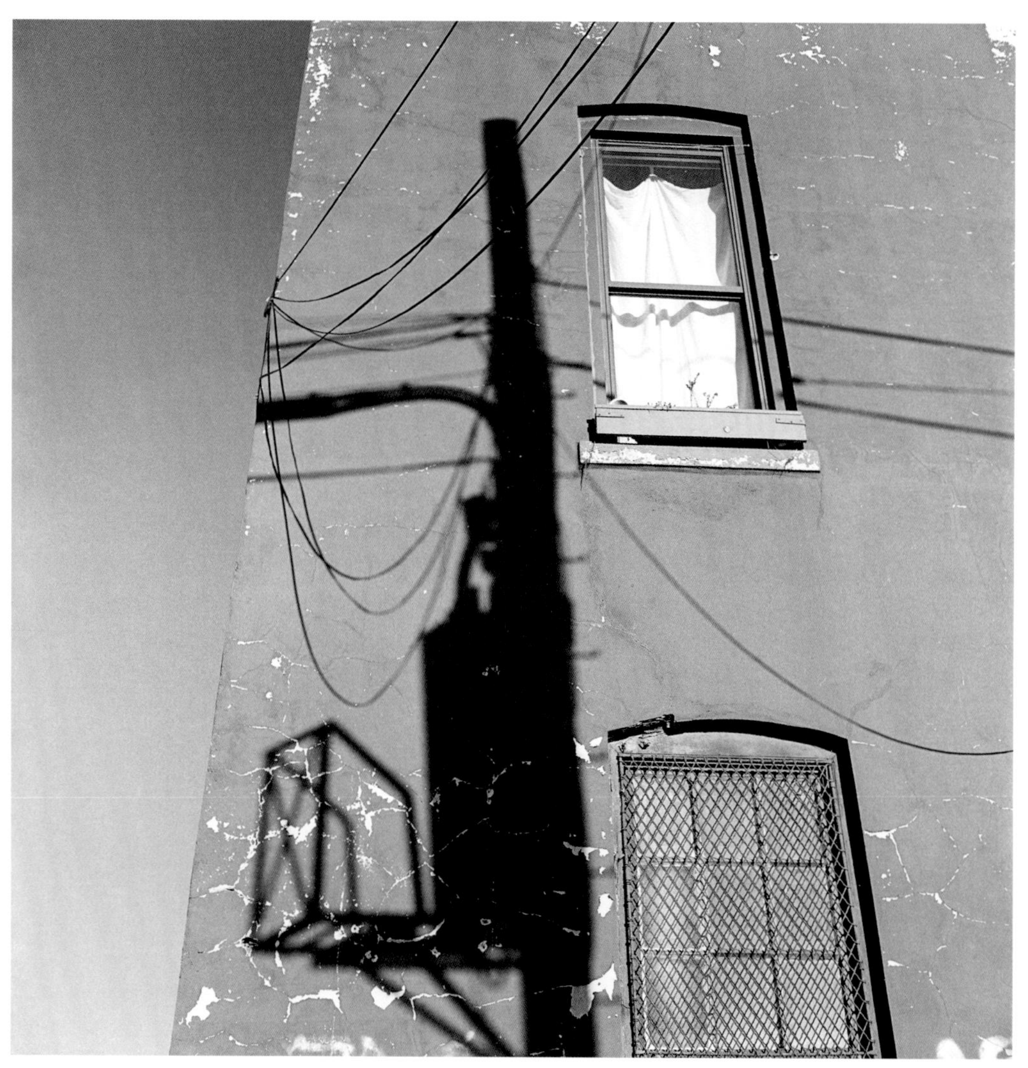

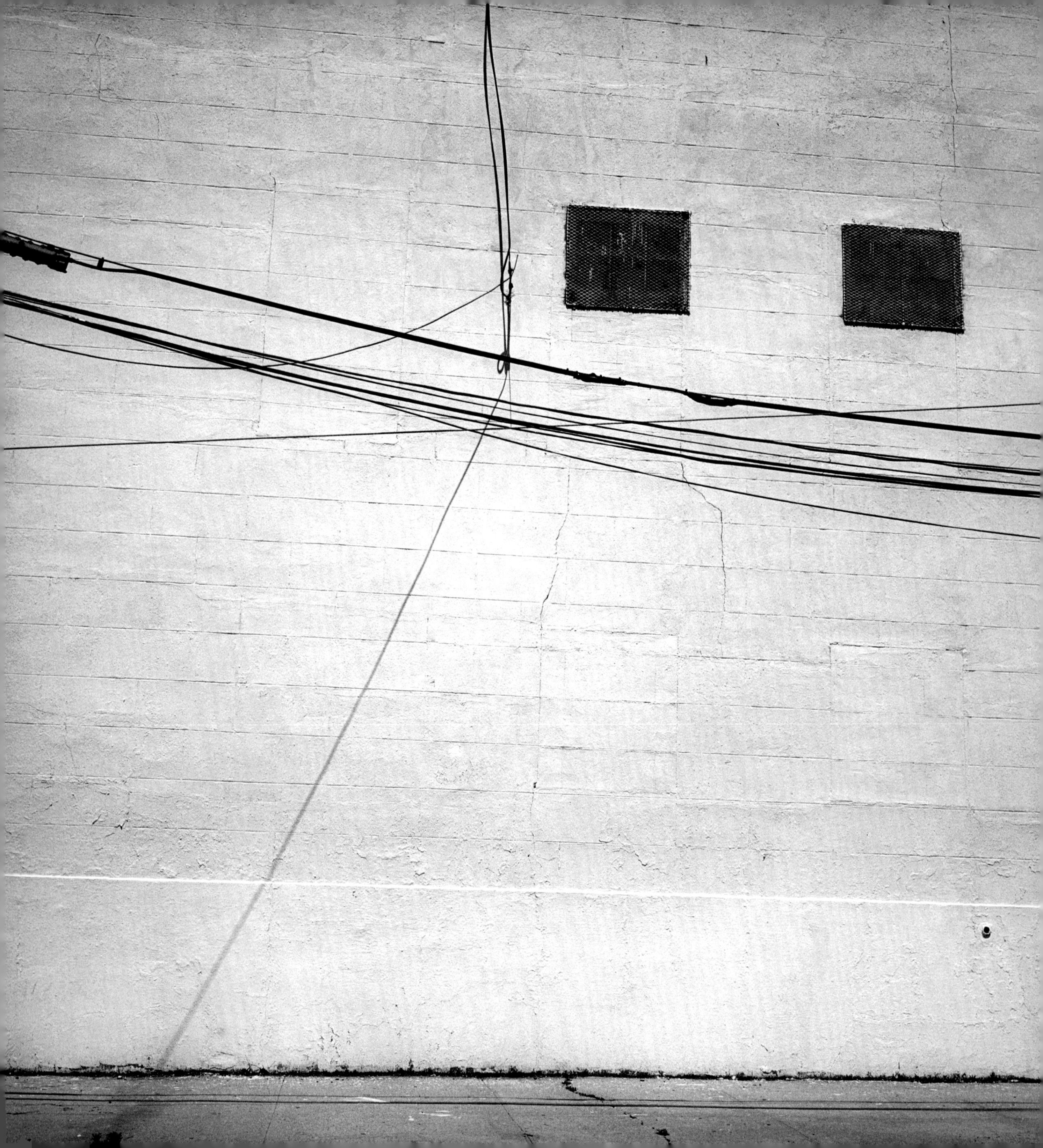

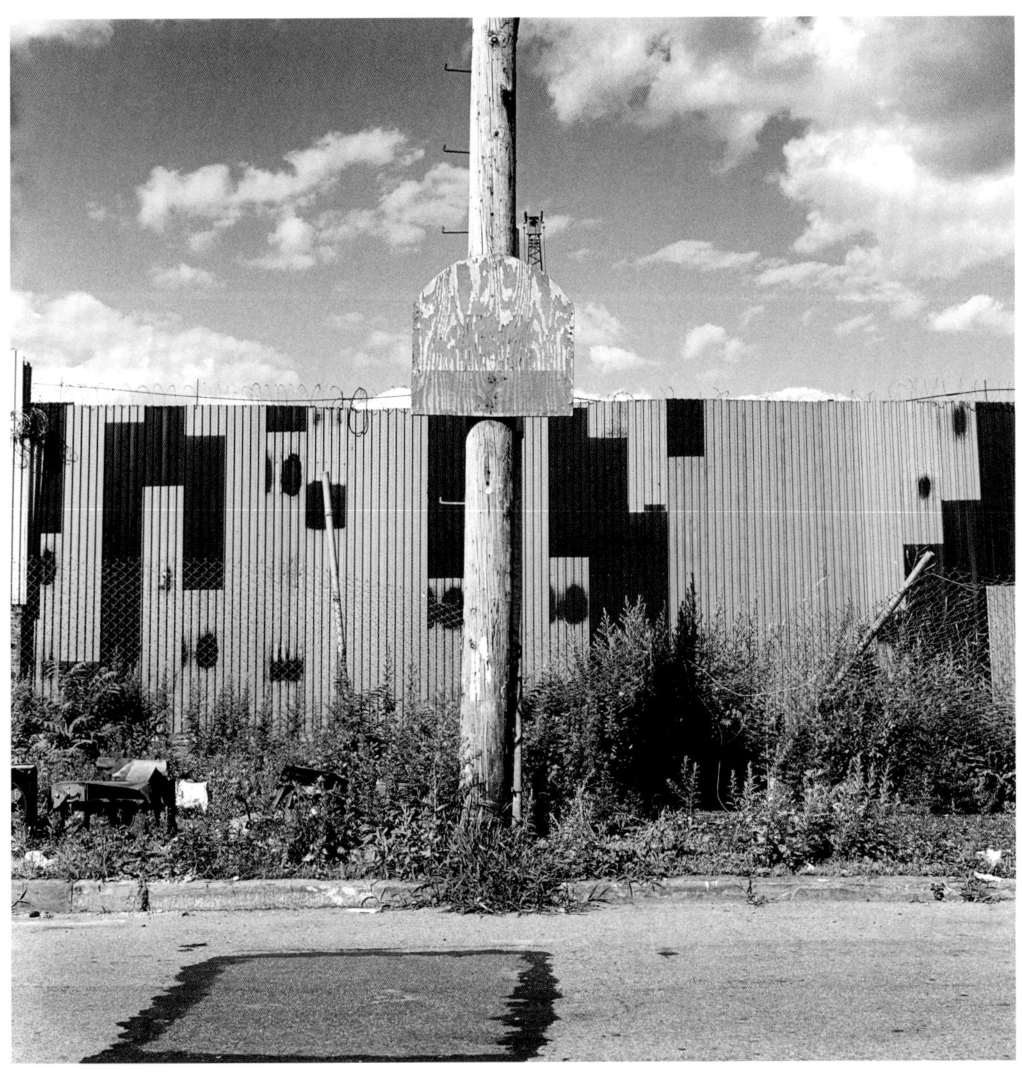

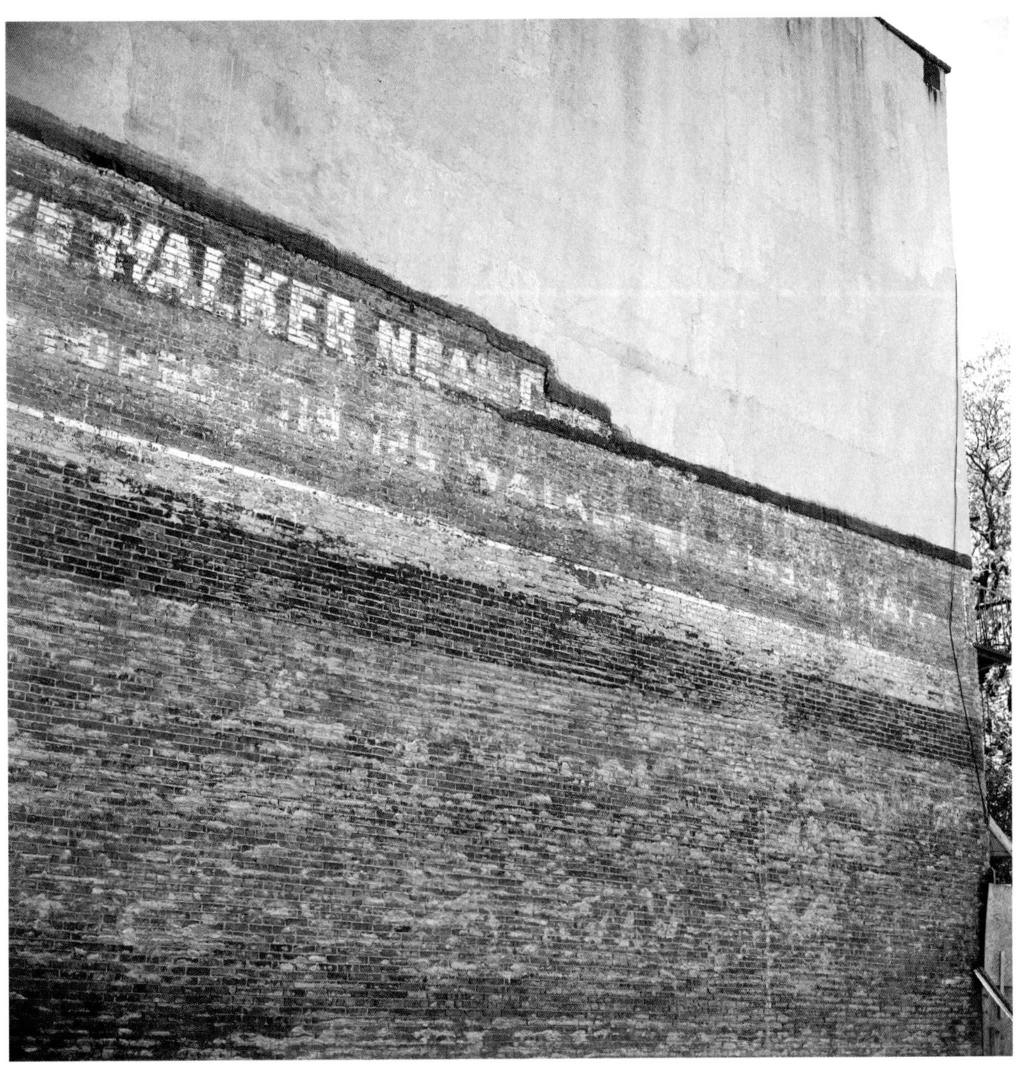
WALKER

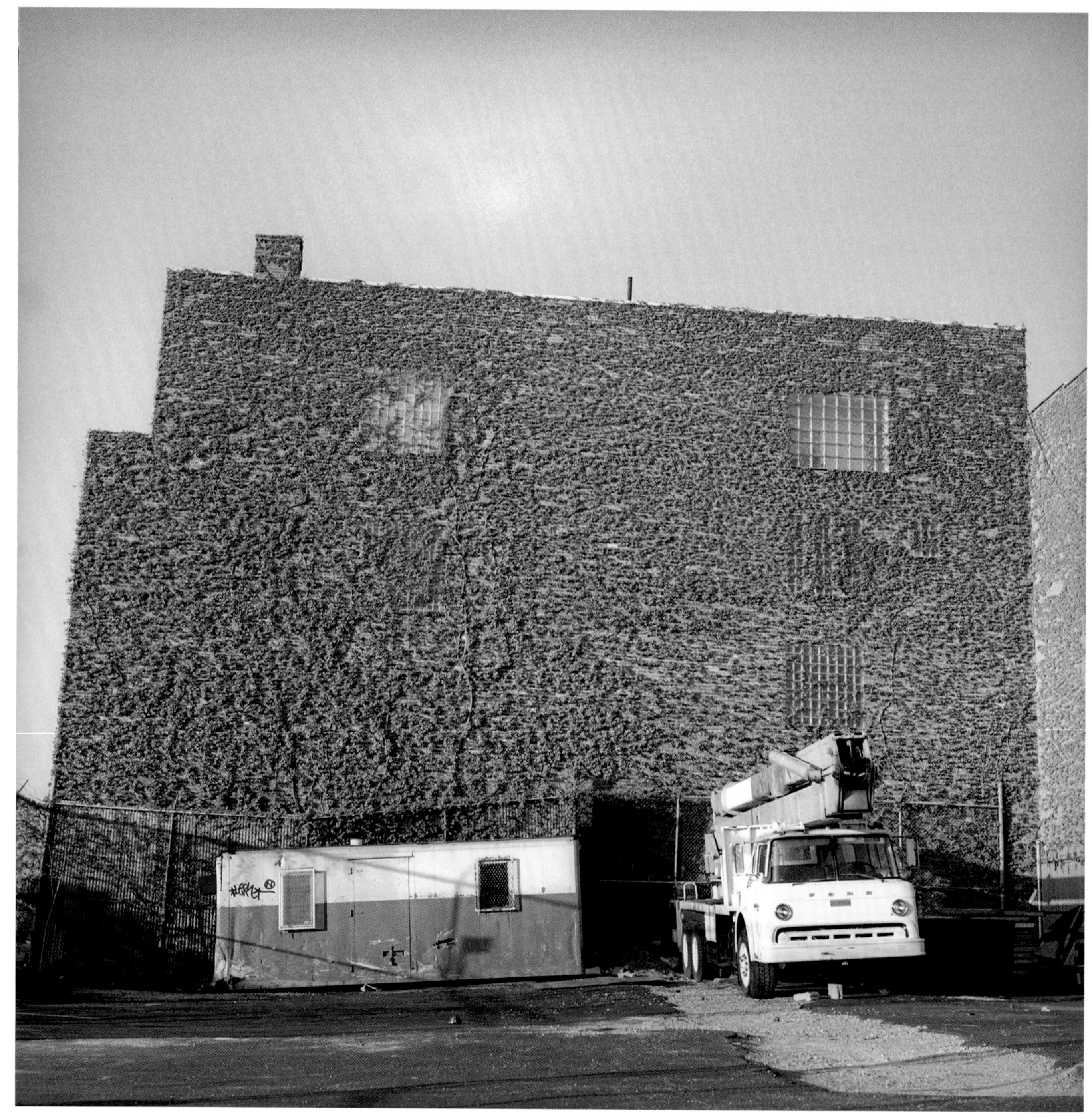

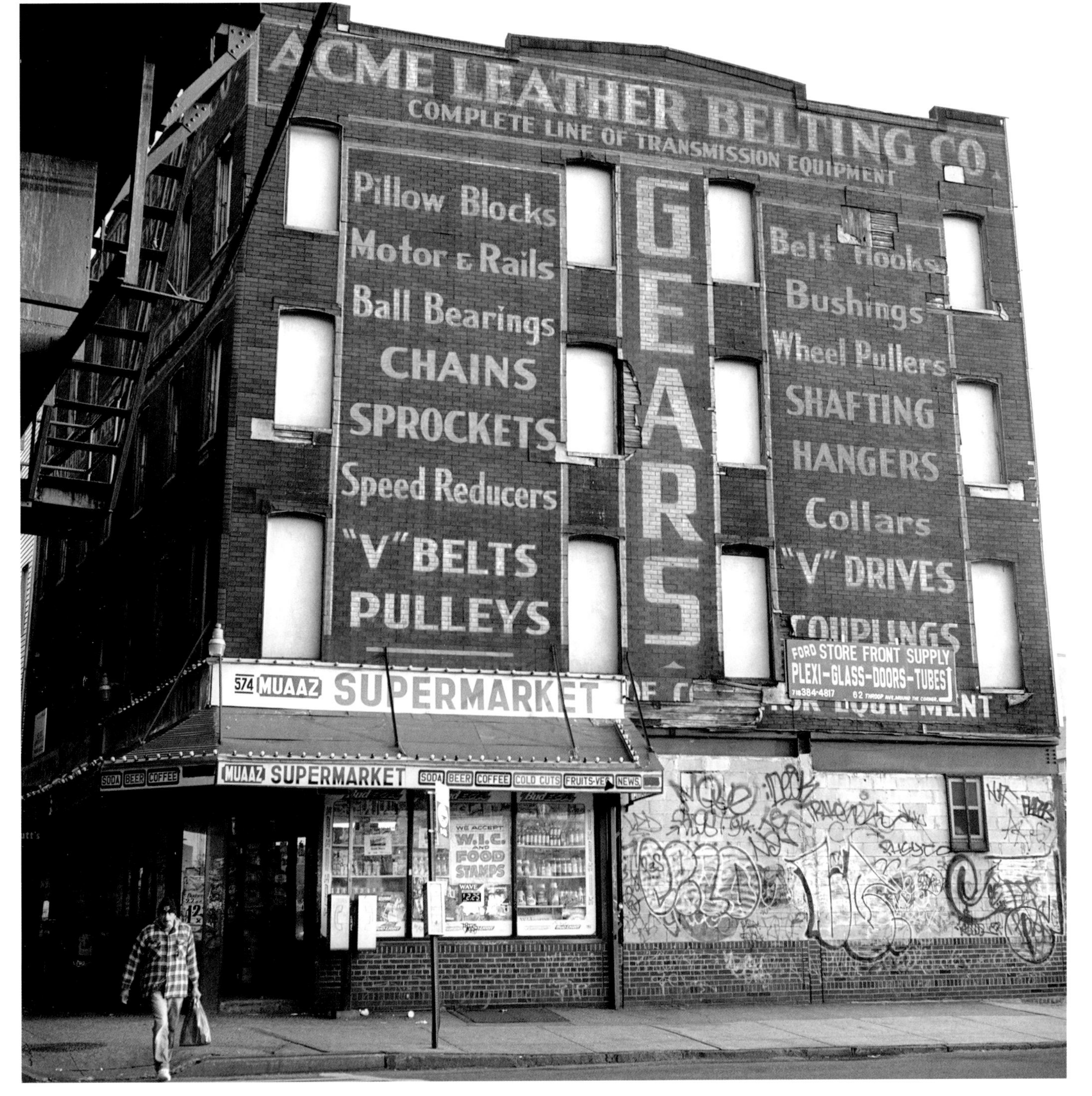
ACME LEATHER BELTING CO.
COMPLETE LINE OF TRANSMISSION EQUIPMENT
Pillow Blocks
Motor & Rails
Ball Bearings
CHAINS
SPROCKETS
Speed Reducers
"V" BELTS
PULLEYS
GEARS
Belt Hooks
Bushings
Wheel Pullers
SHAFTING
HANGERS
Collars
"V" DRIVES
COUPLINGS
FORD STORE FRONT SUPPLY
PLEXI-GLASS-DOORS-TUBES
574 MUAAZ SUPERMARKET
MUAAZ SUPERMARKET
SODA BEER COFFEE
SODA BEER COFFEE COLD CUTS FRUITS-VEG NEWS
WE ACCEPT W.I.C. AND FOOD STAMPS

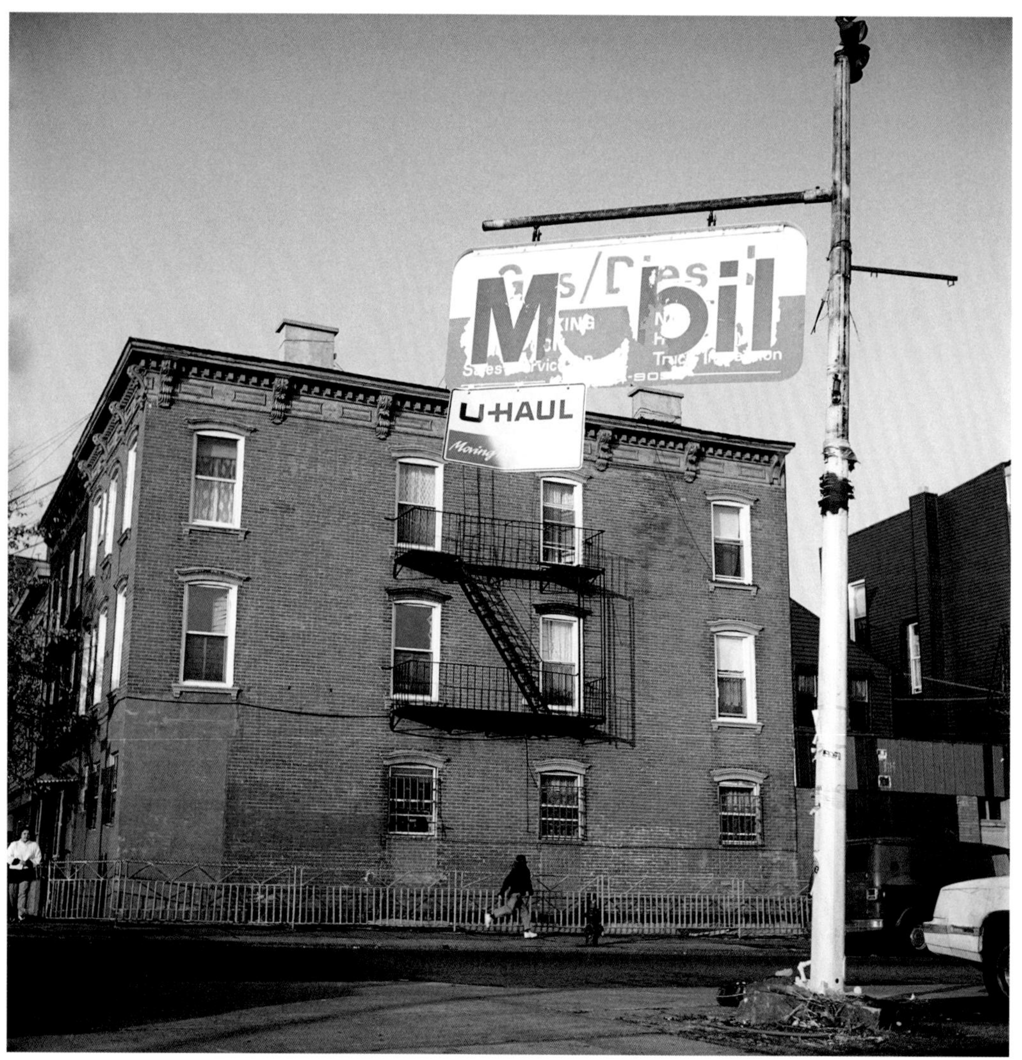
Mobil
U-HAUL

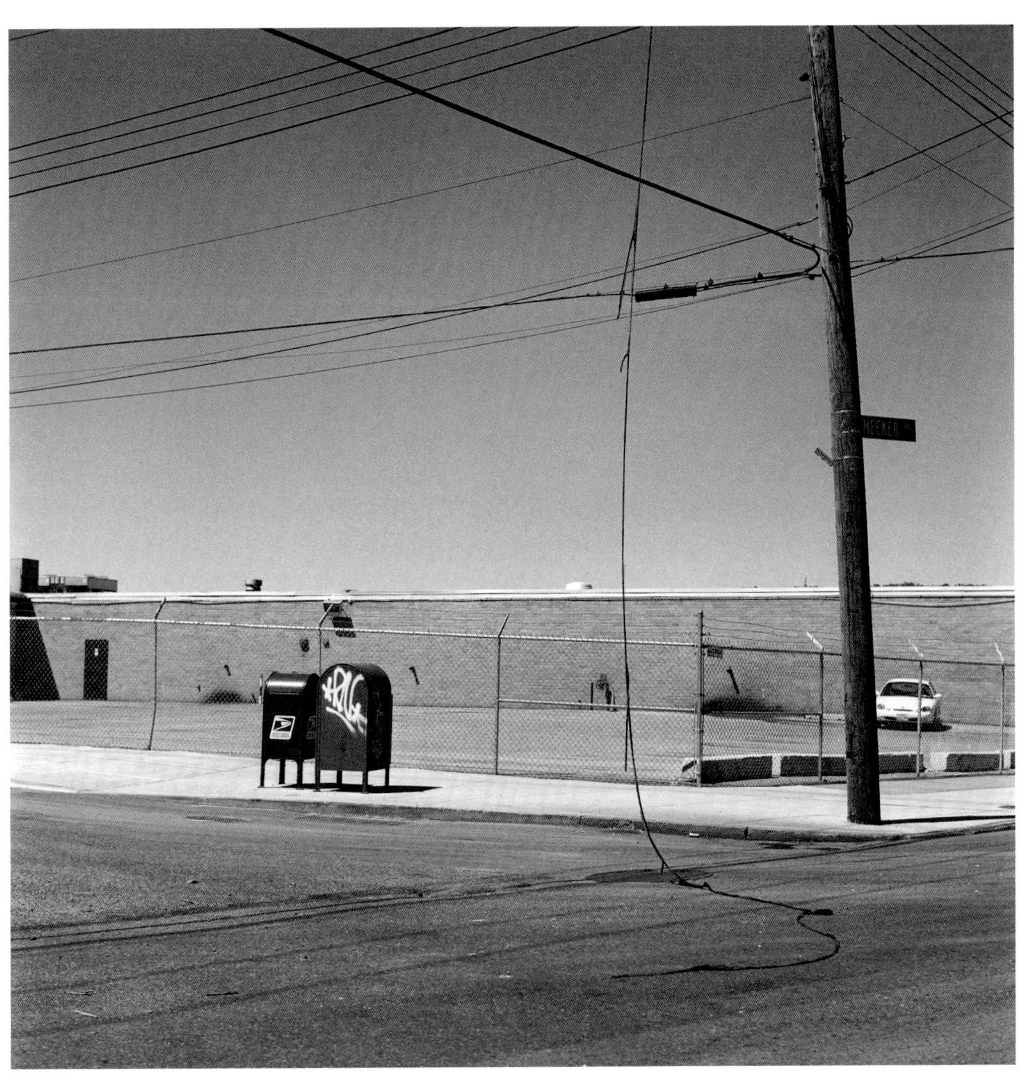

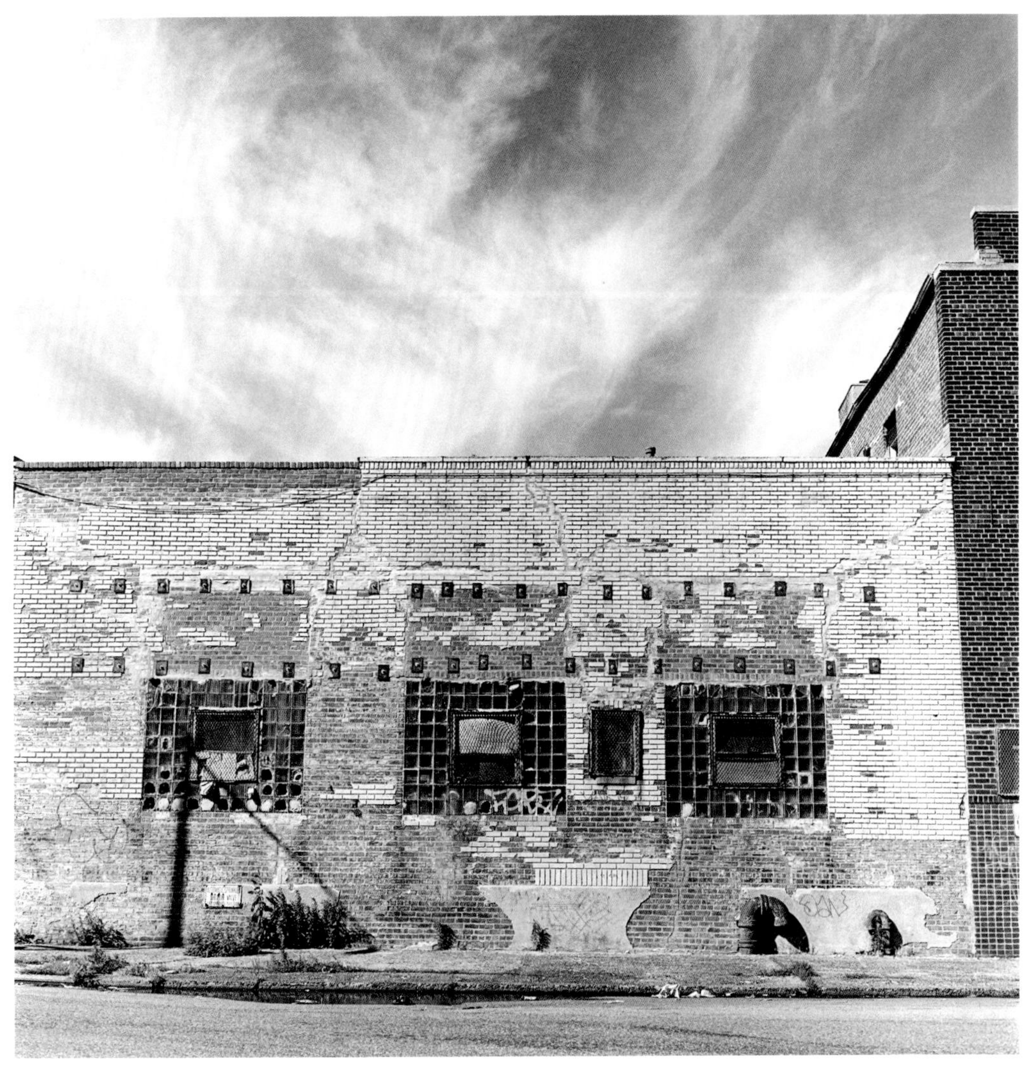

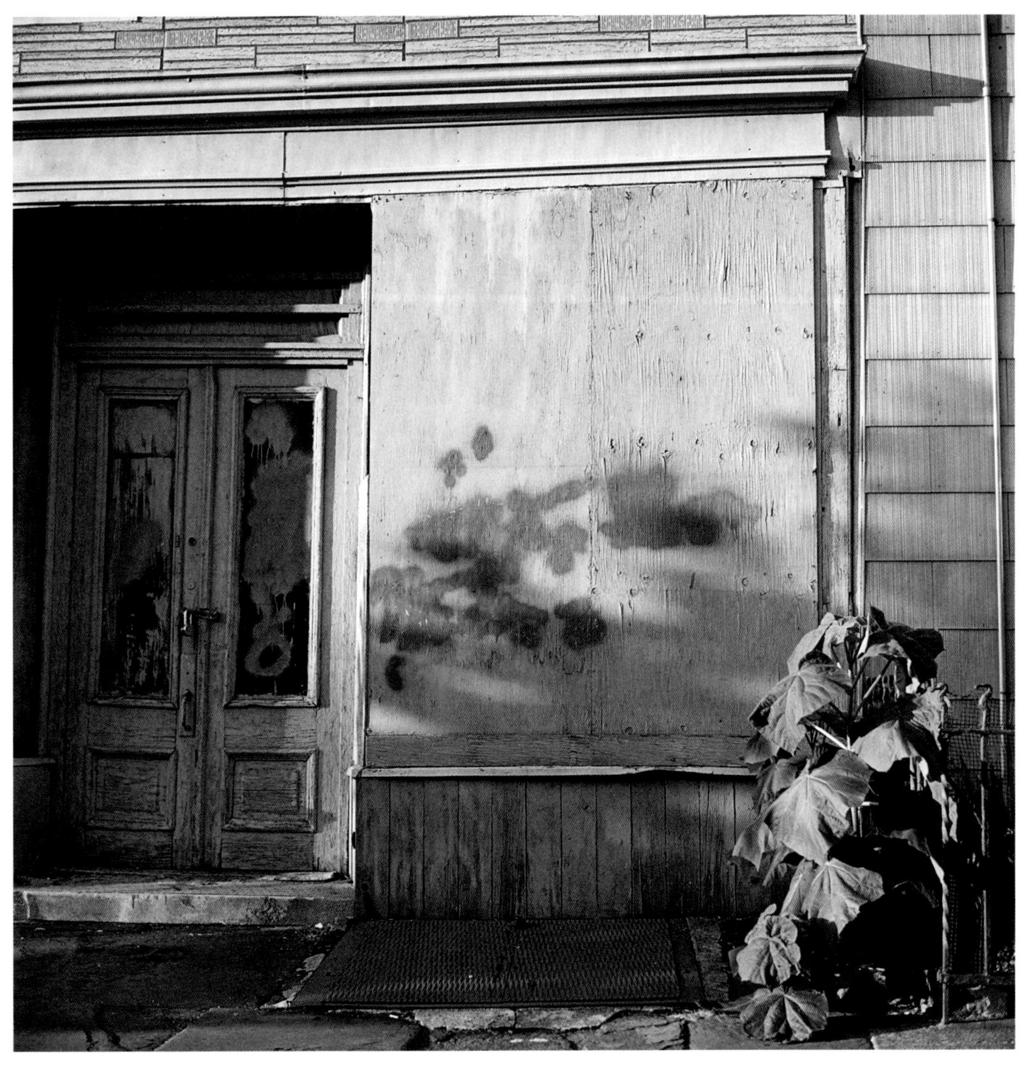

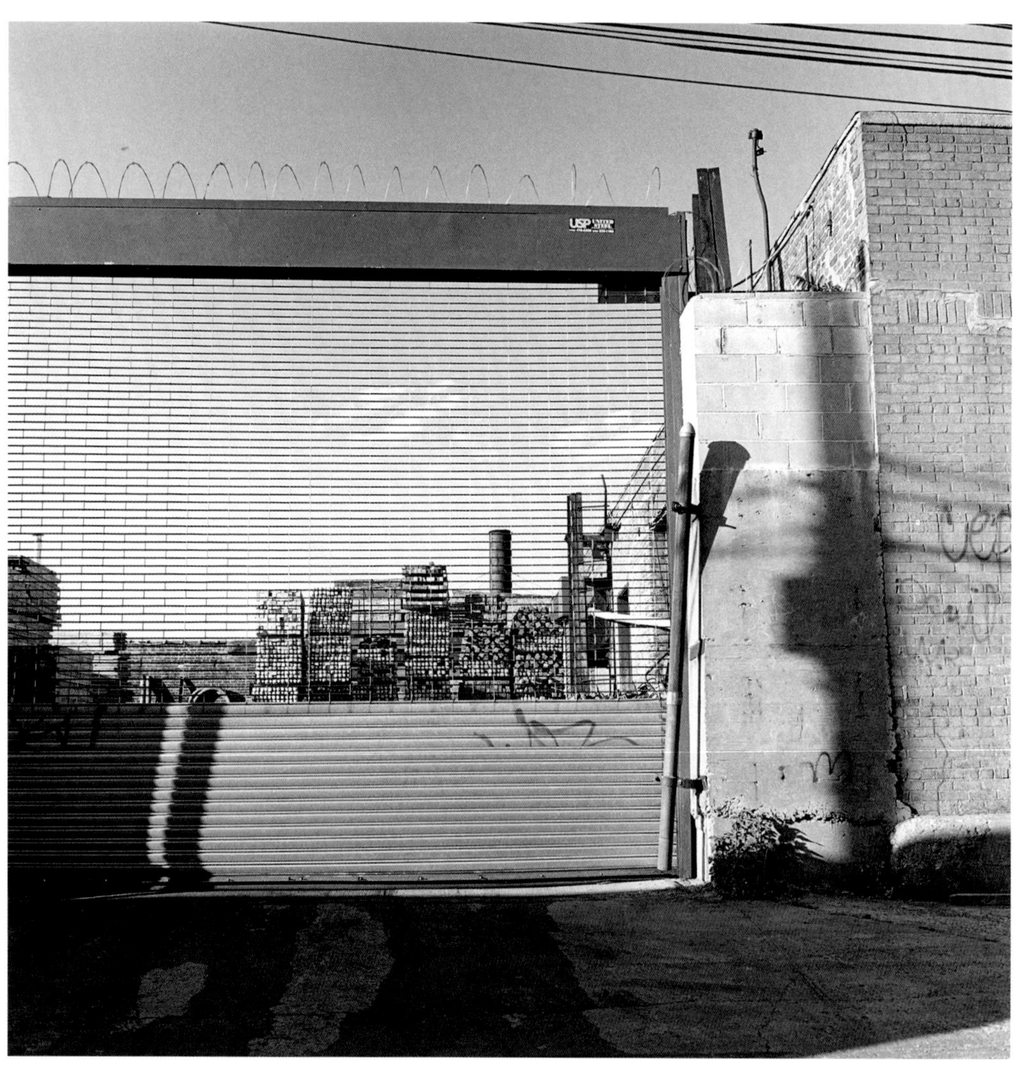
USP

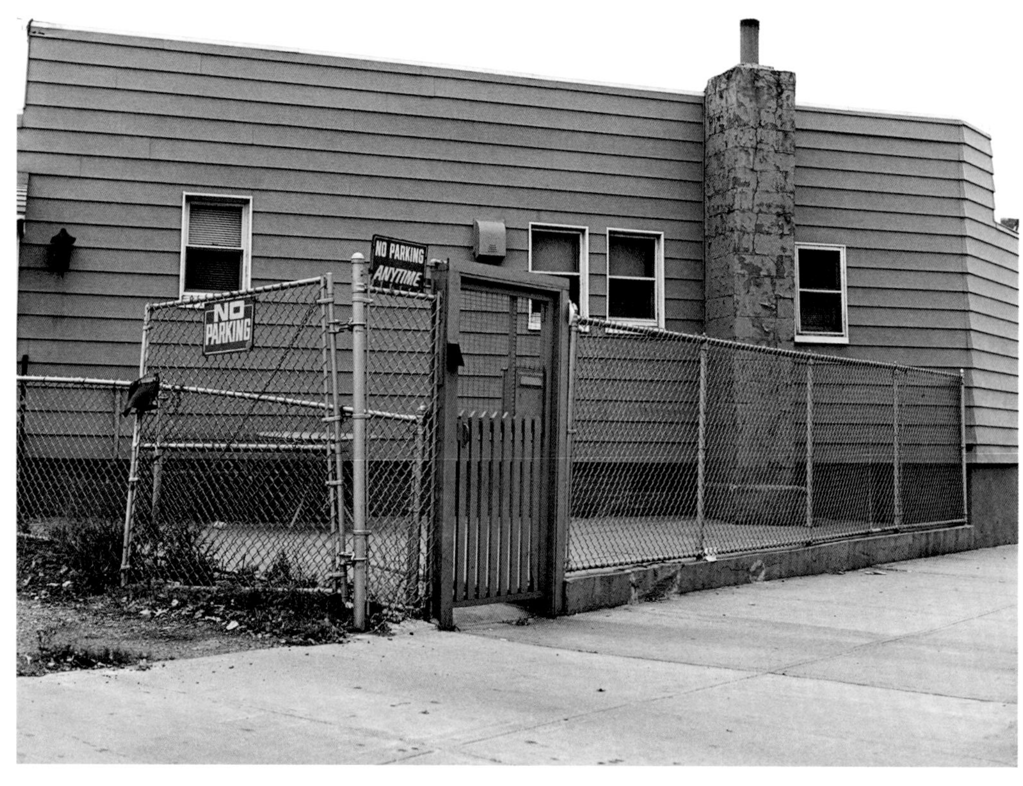
NO PARKING
ANYTIME
NO
PARKING

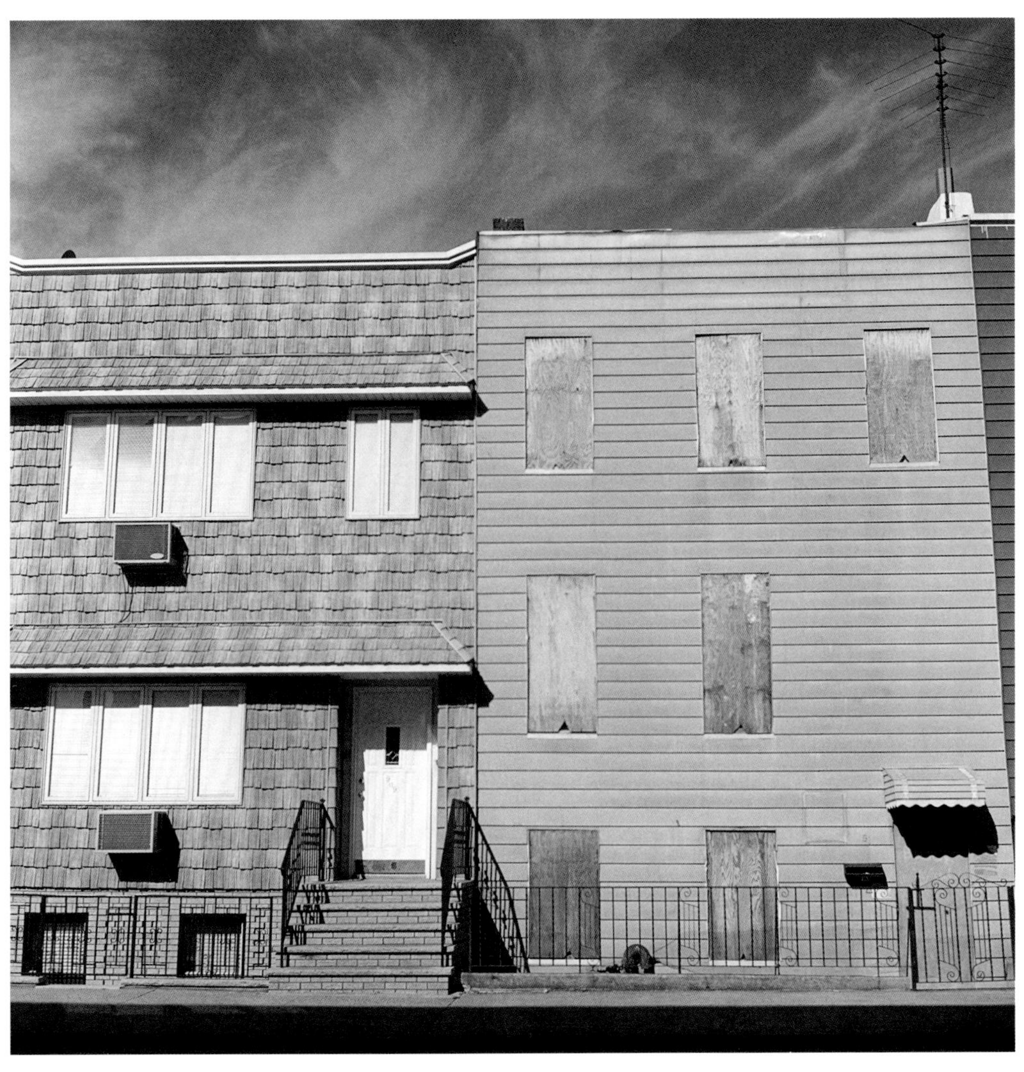

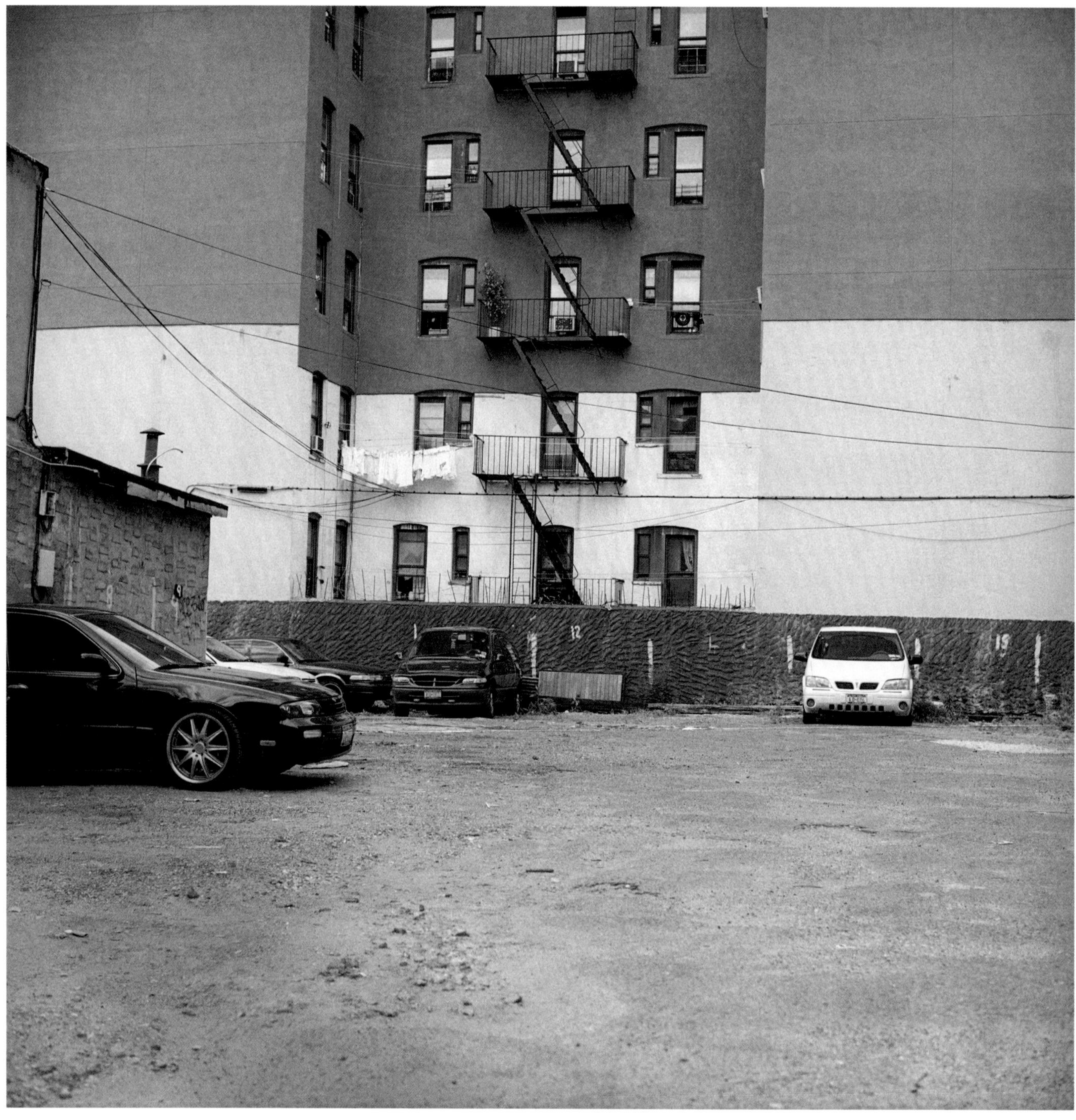
12
19

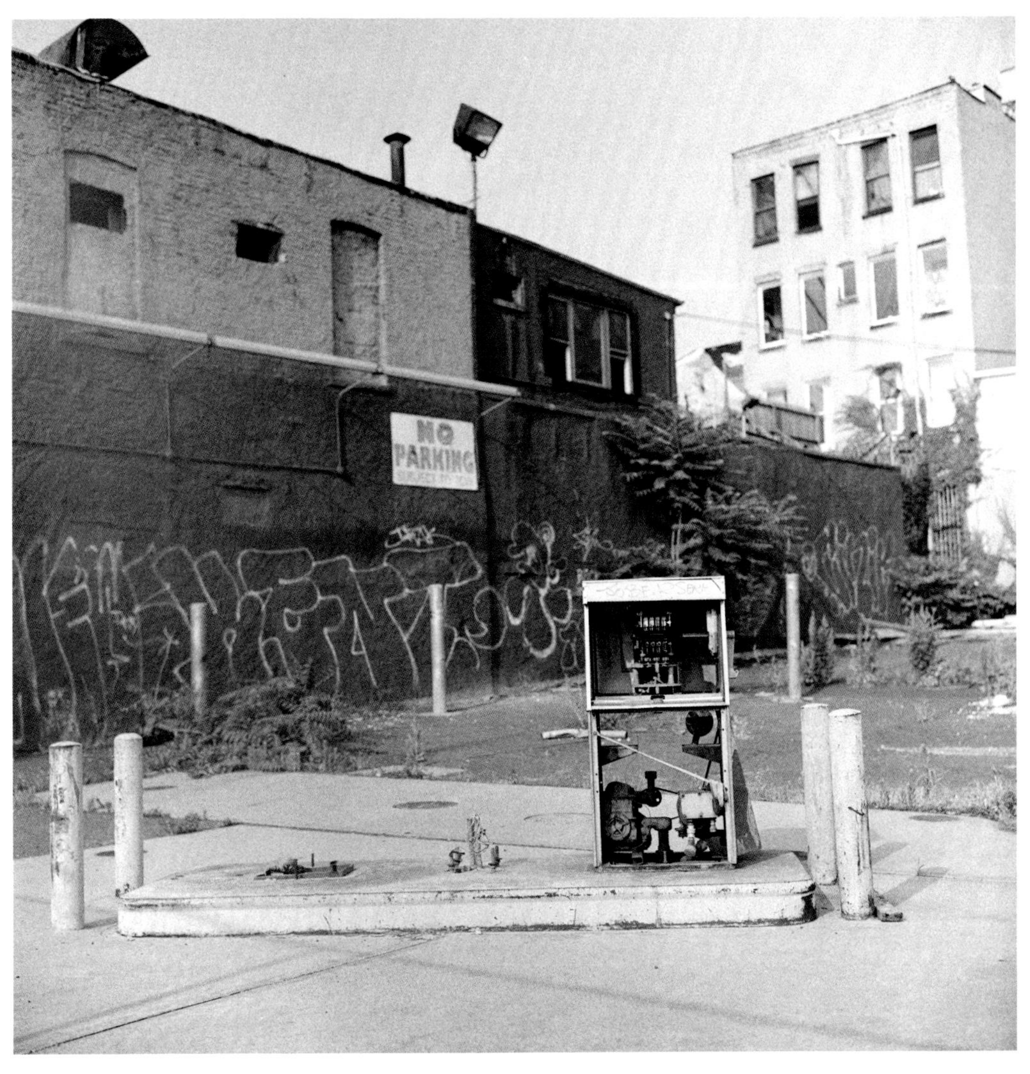
NO
PARKING

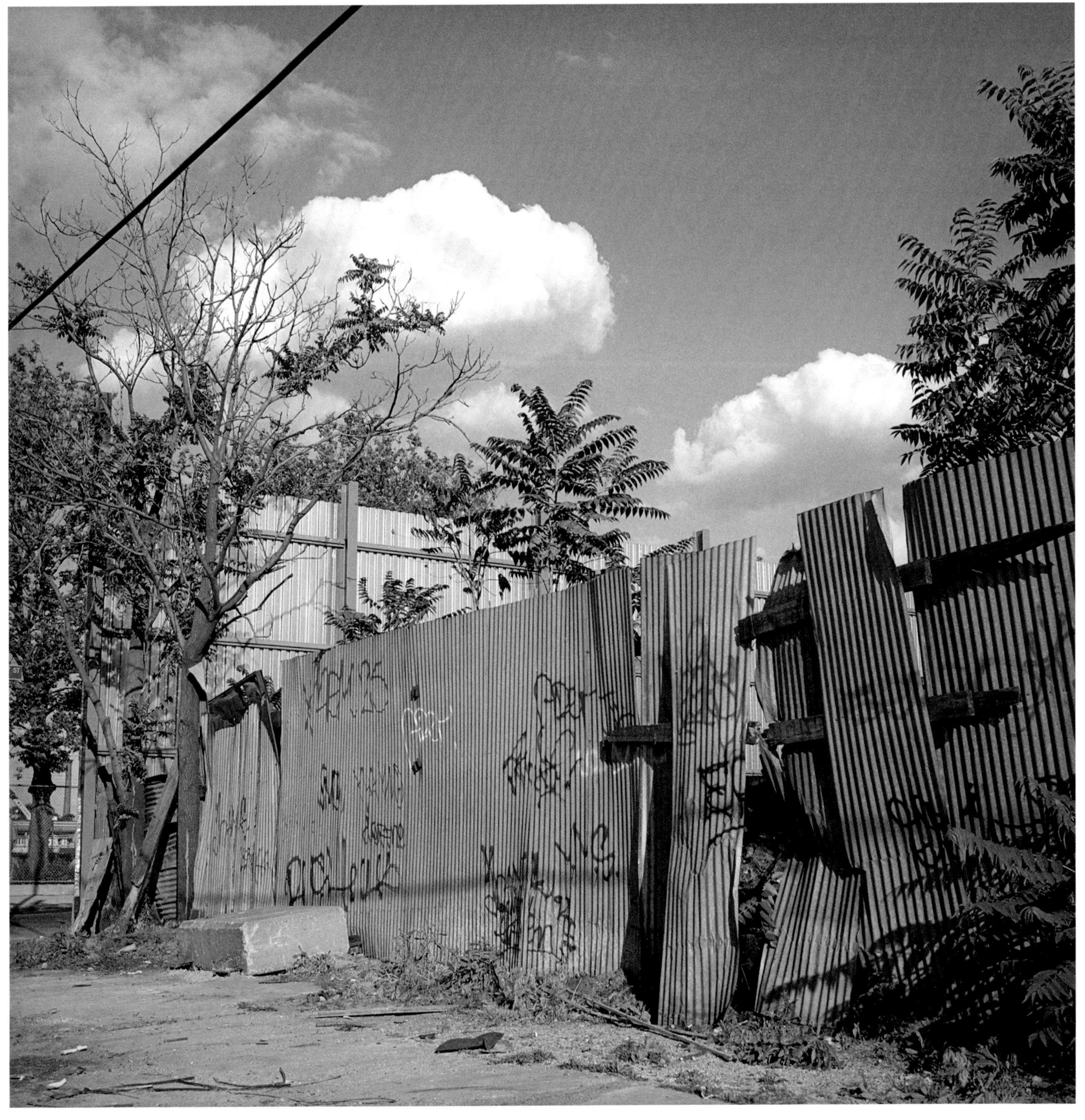

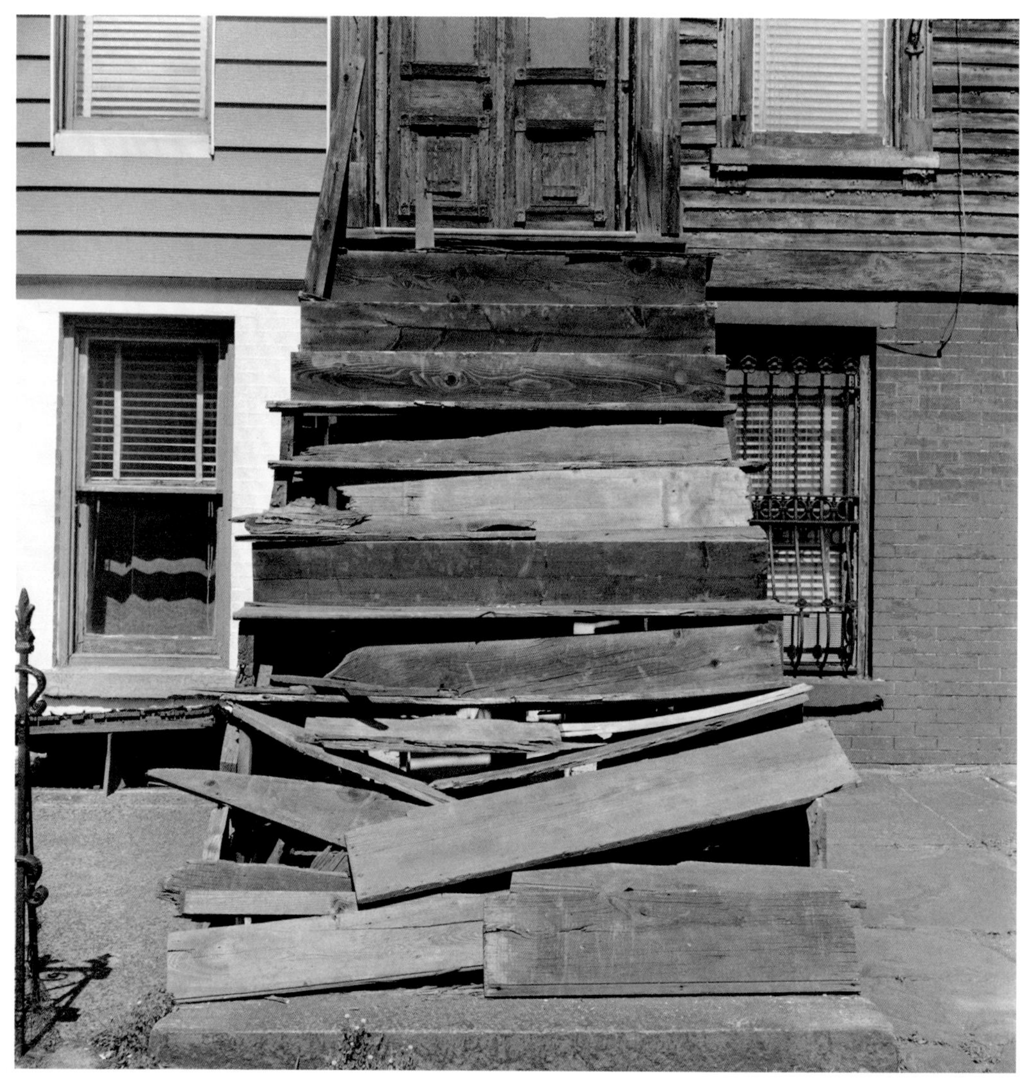

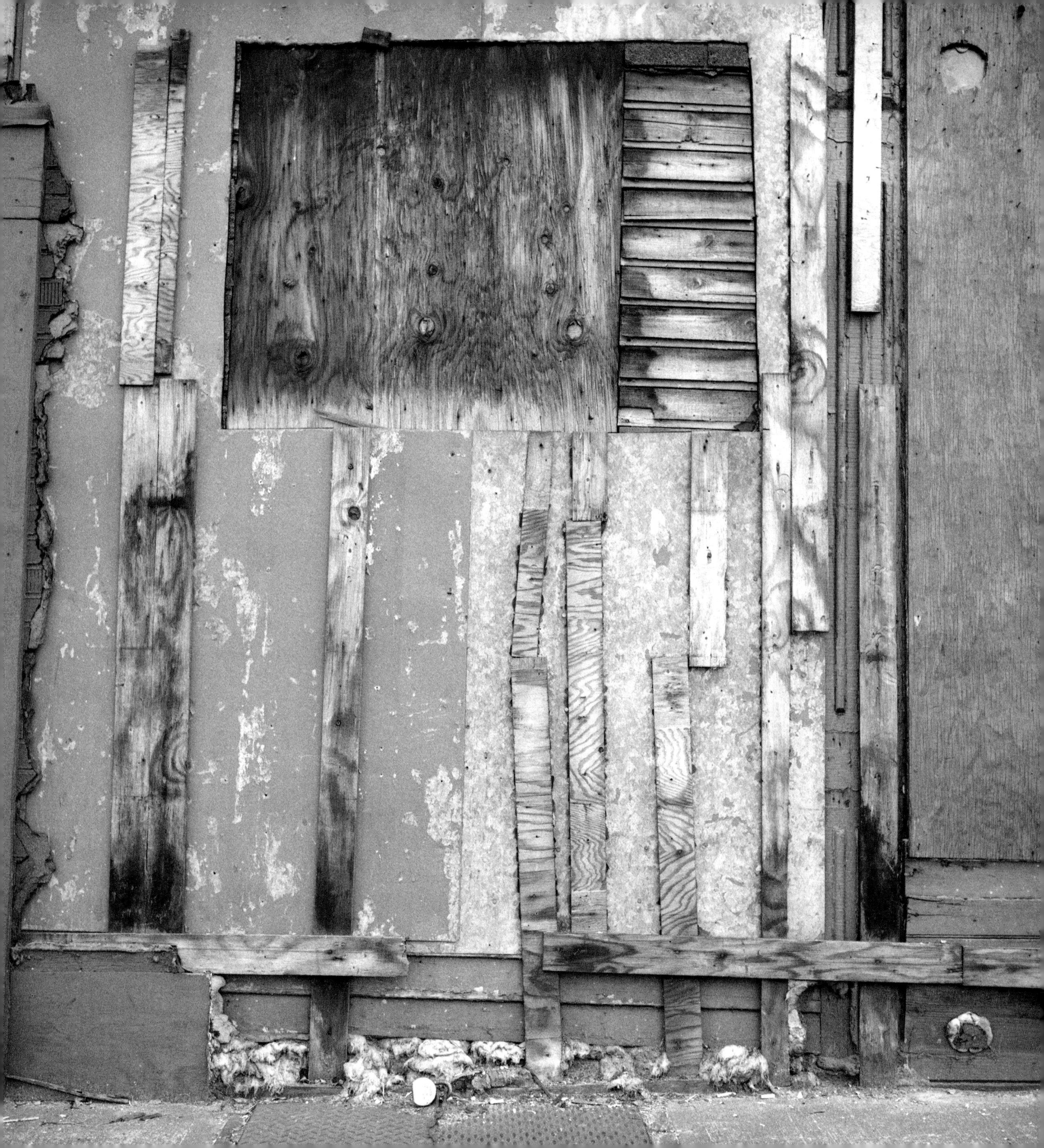

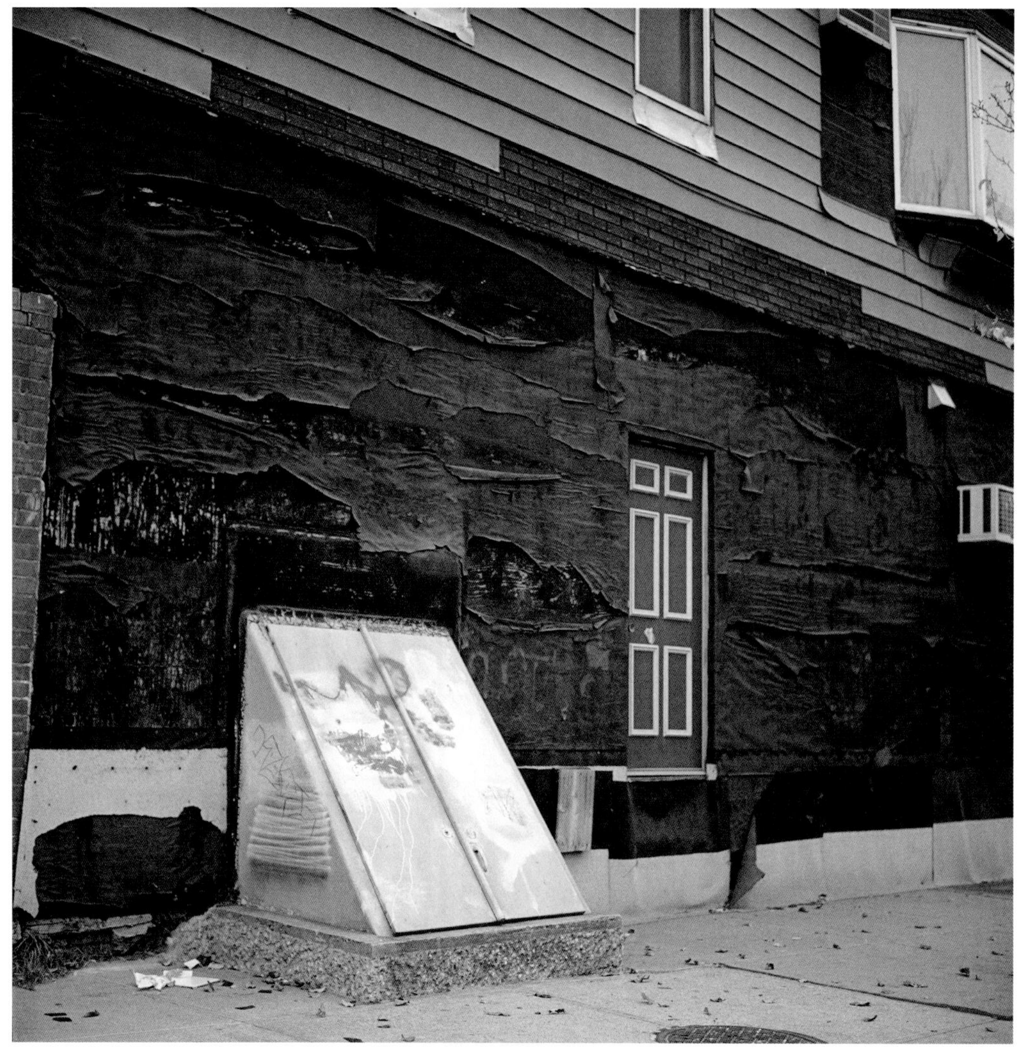

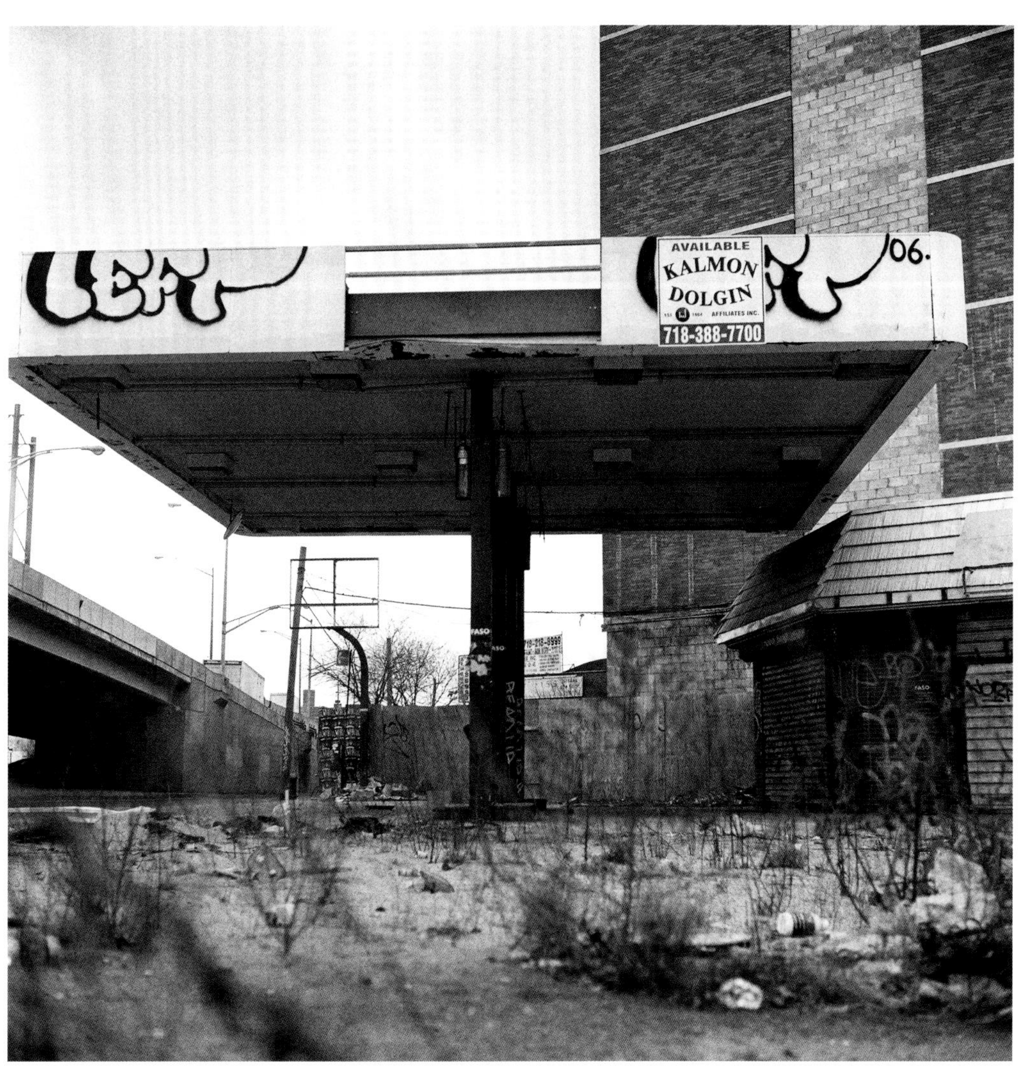
AVAILABLE
KALMON
DOLGIN
AFFILIATES INC.
718-388-7700
06.

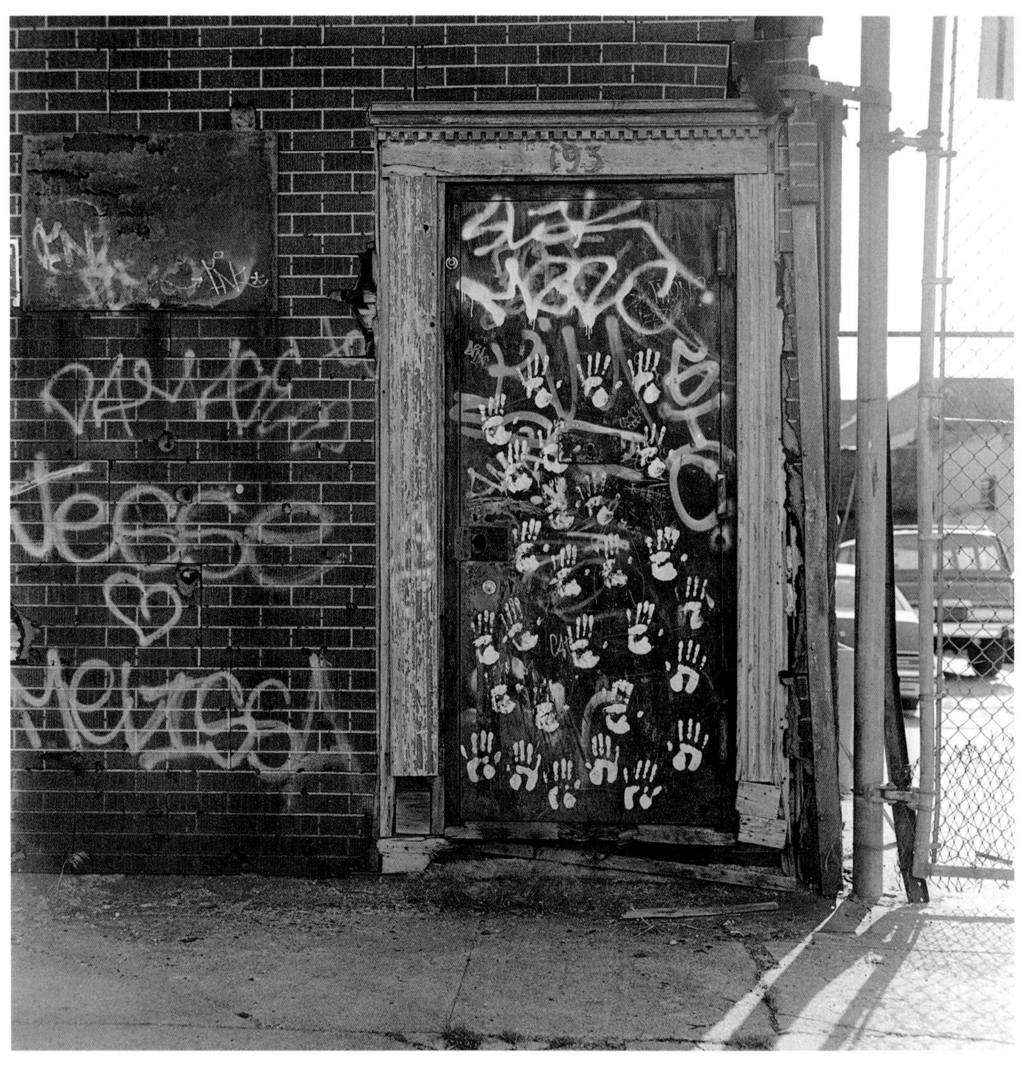
193
Jesse
Melissa

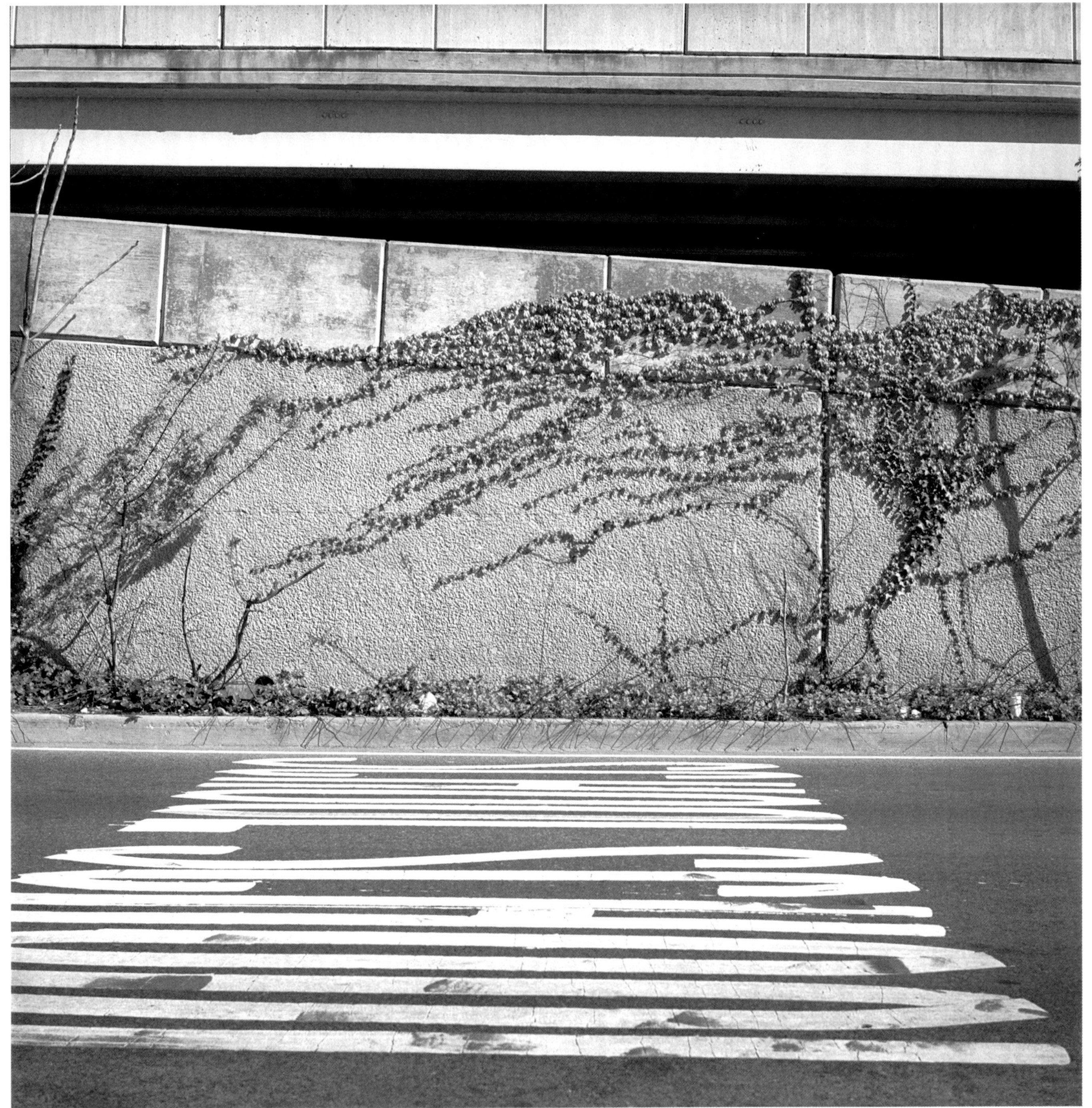

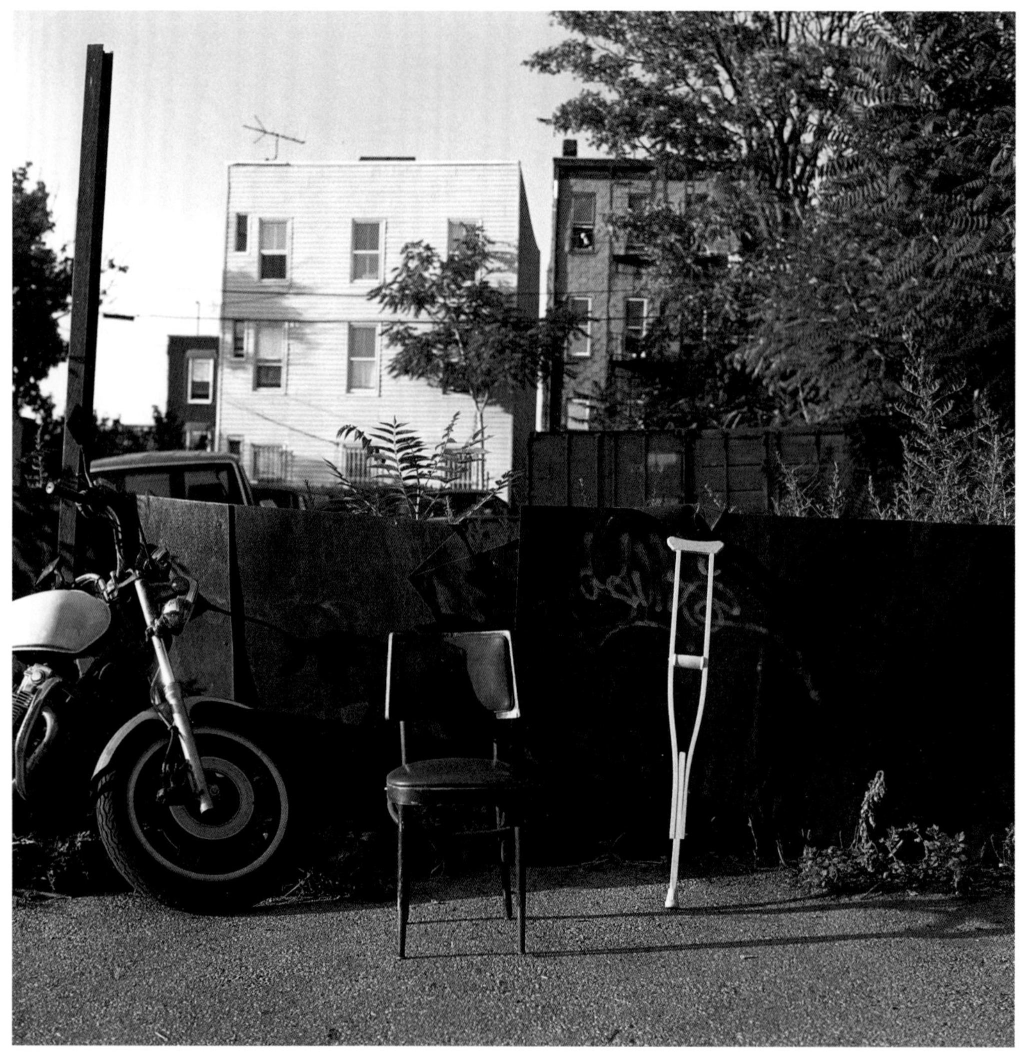

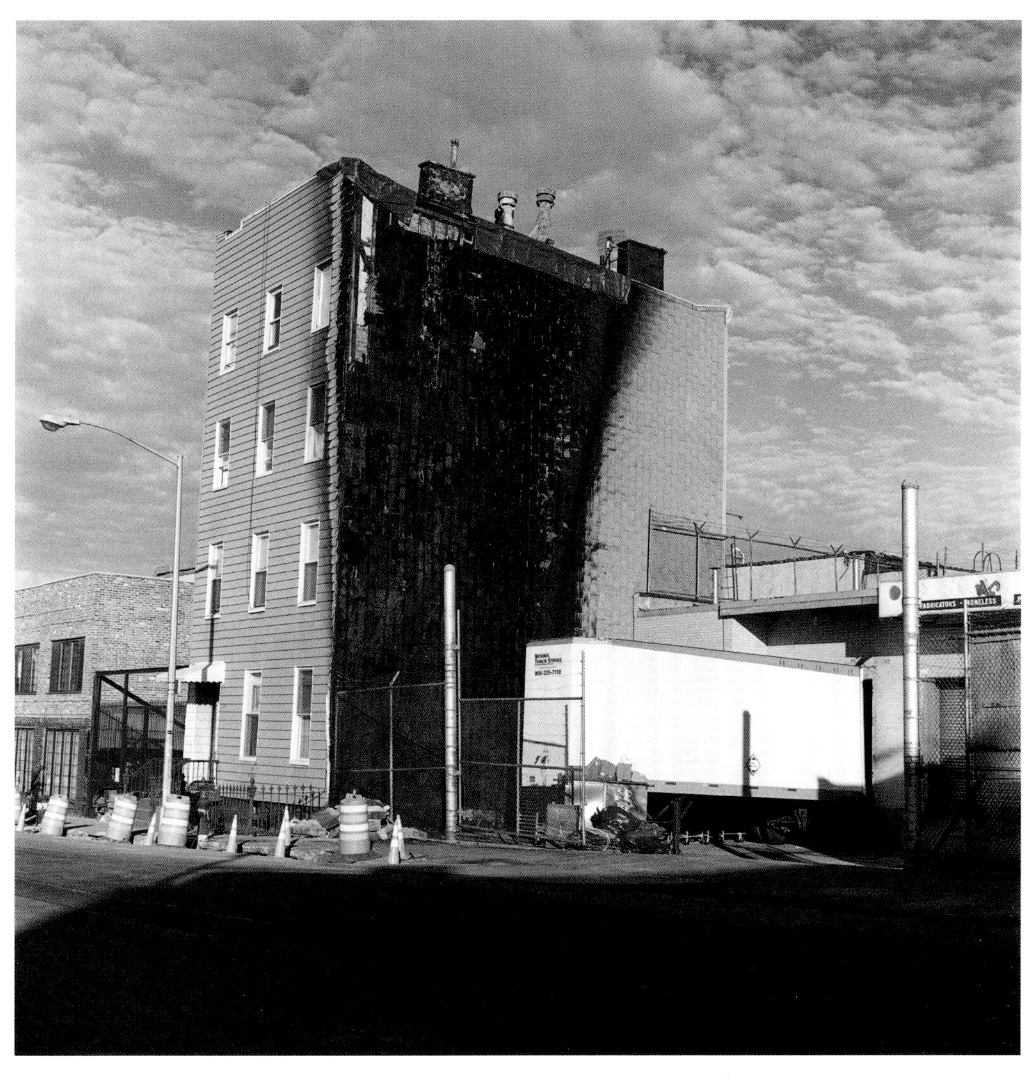

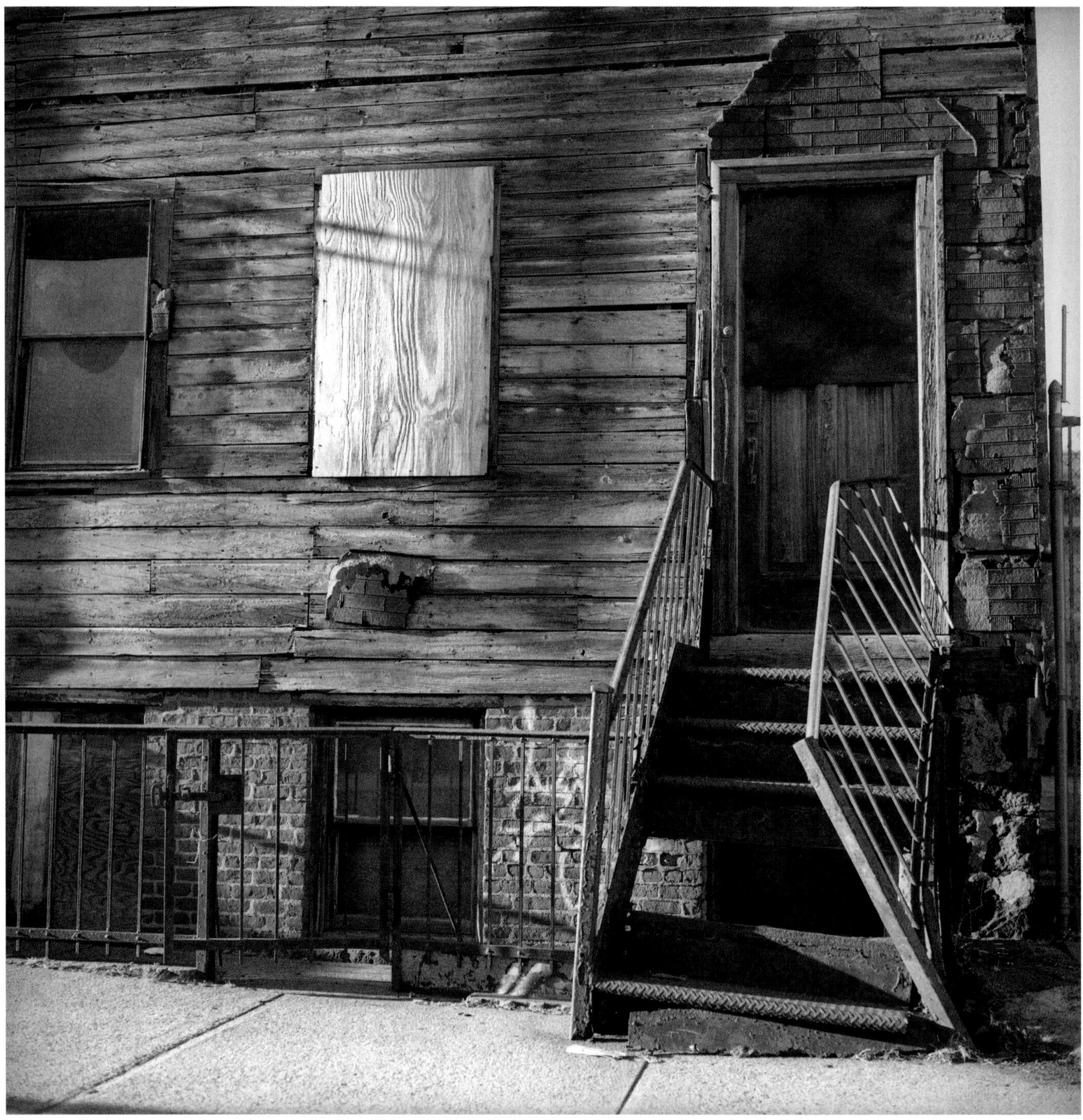

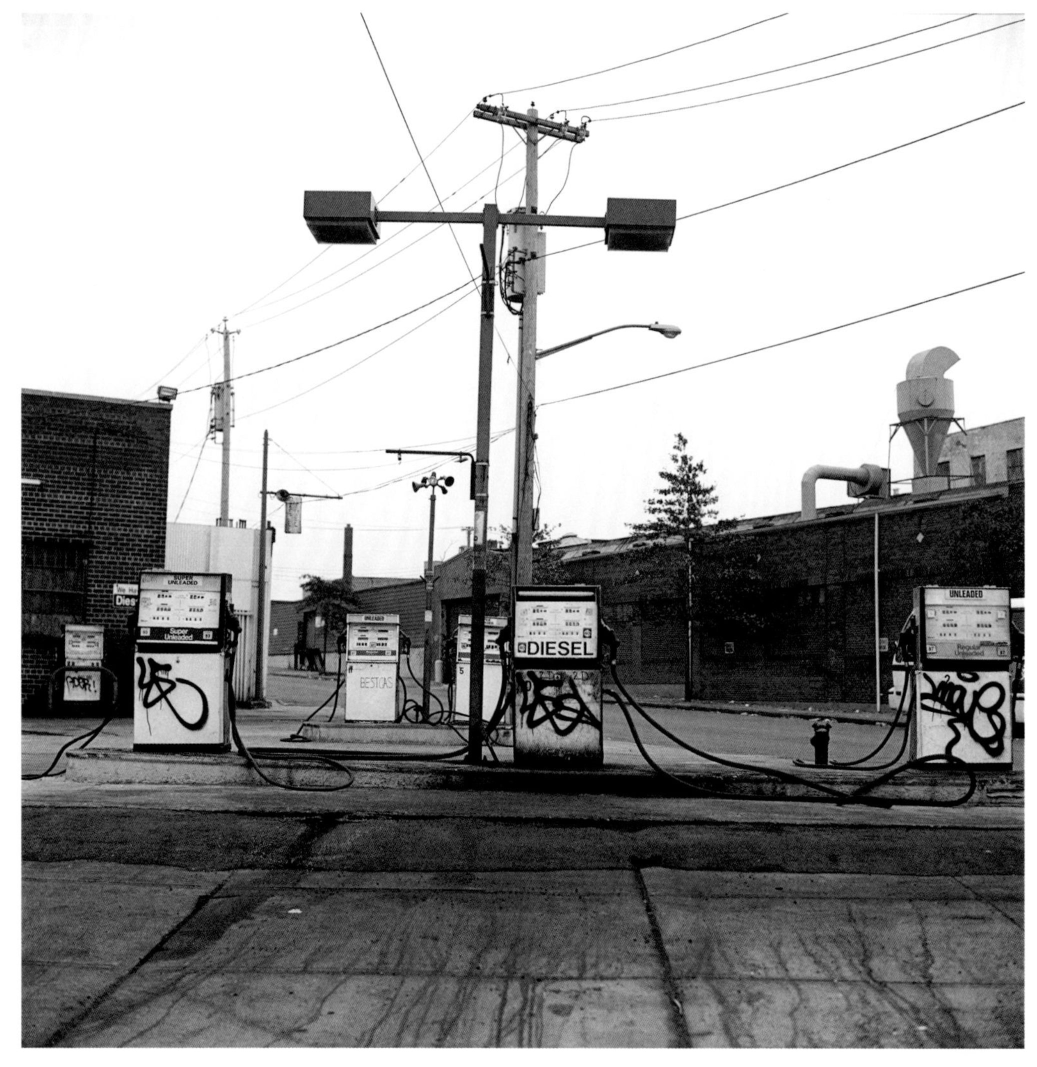
SUPER UNLEADED
DIESEL
UNLEADED

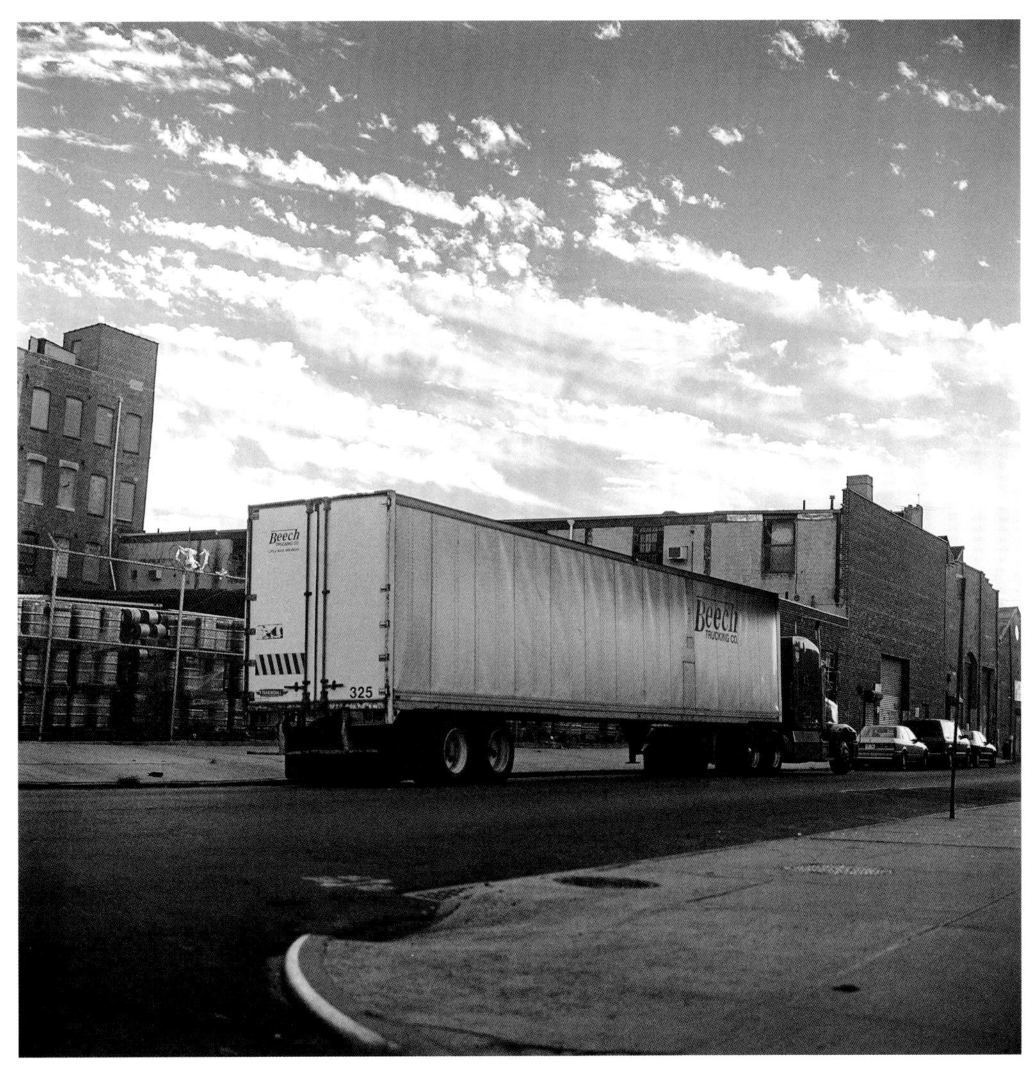
Beech
TRUCKING CO.
325
Beech
TRUCKING CO.

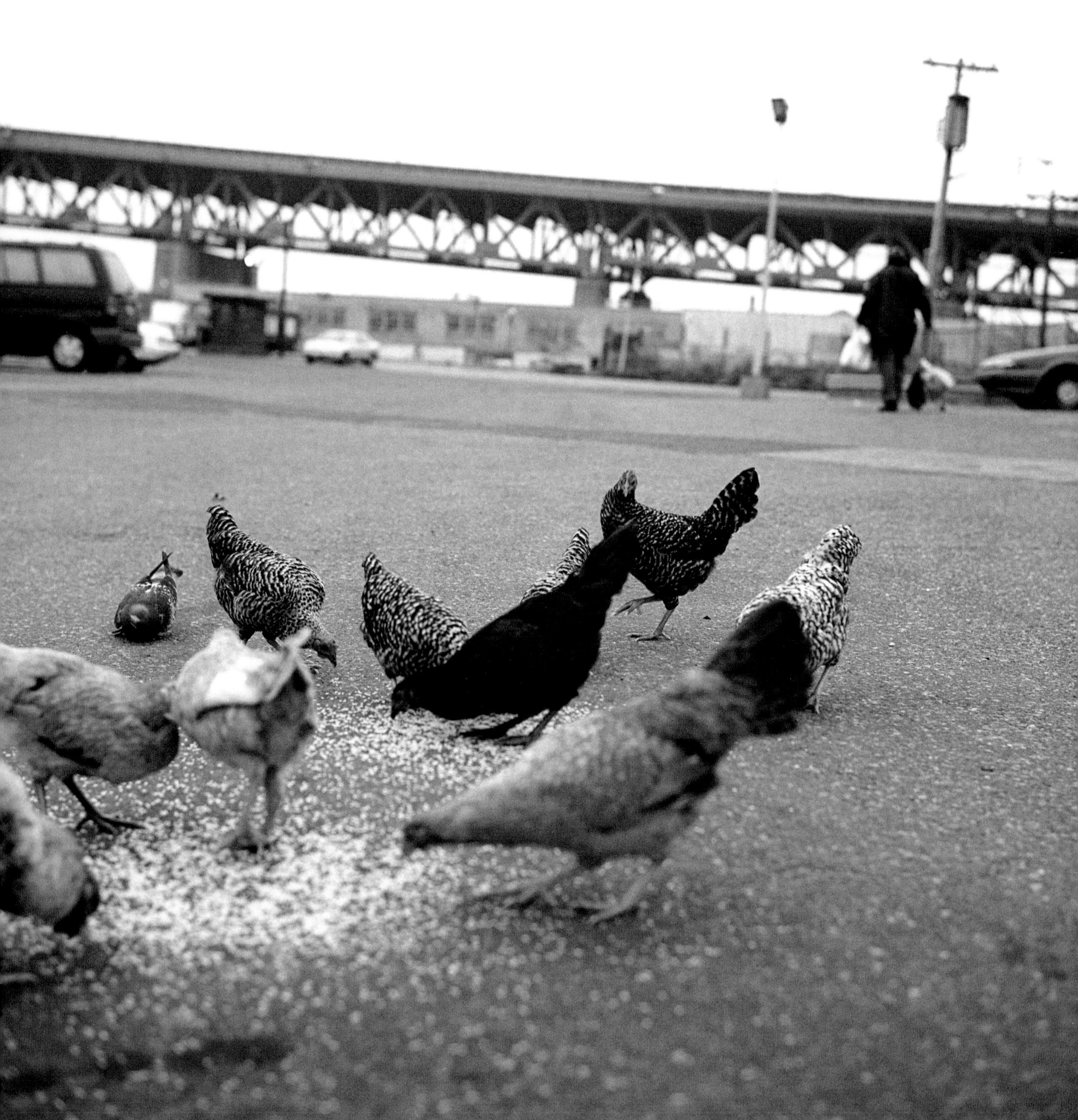

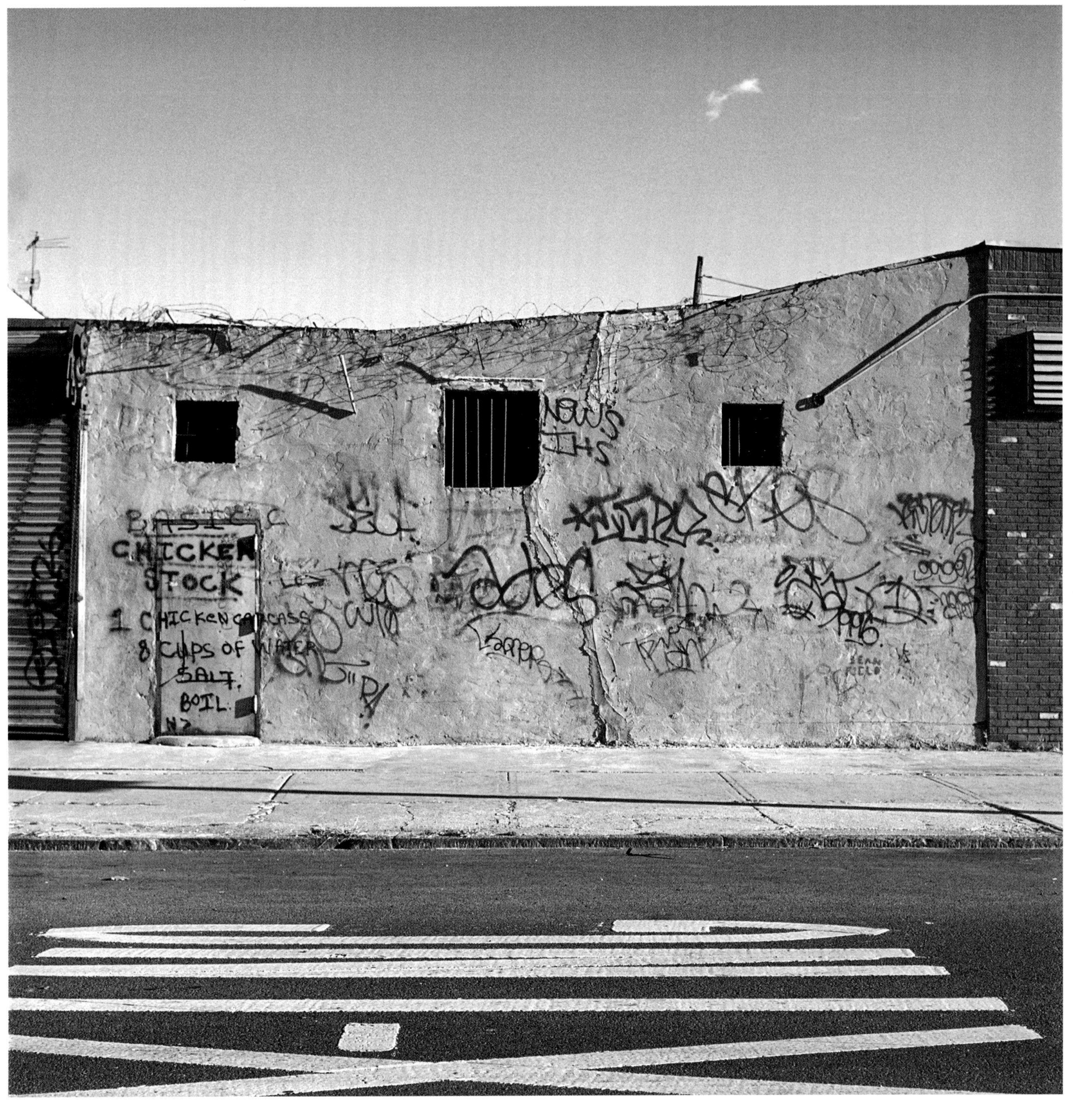
BASIC
CHICKEN
STOCK
1 CHICKEN CARCASS
8 CUPS OF WATER
SALT.
BOIL.

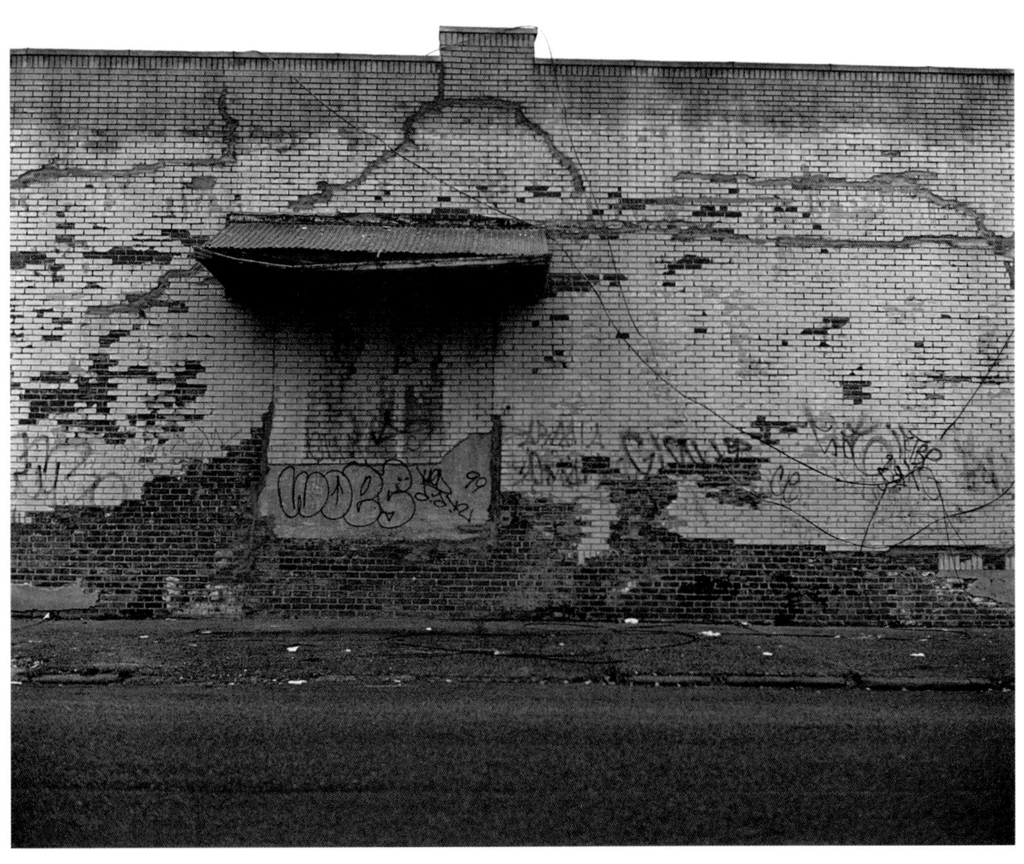

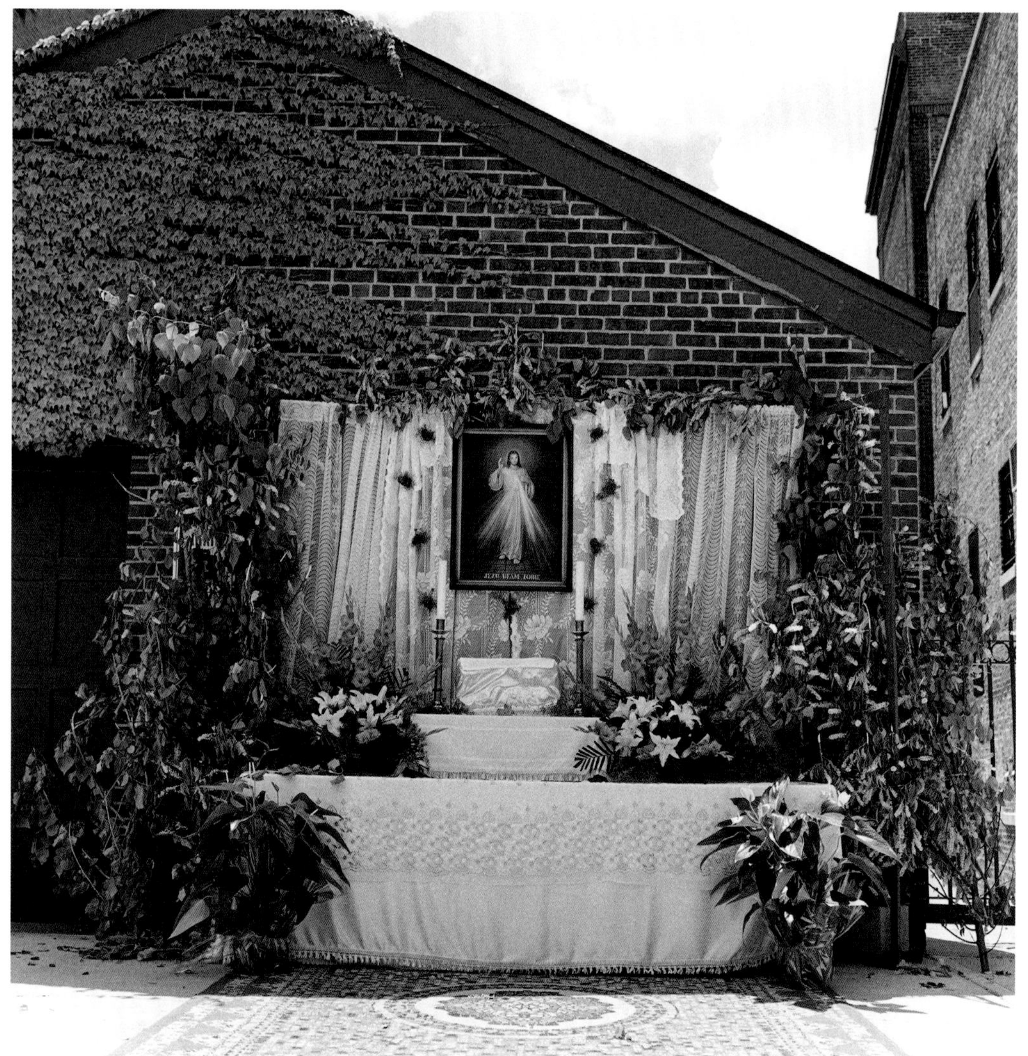

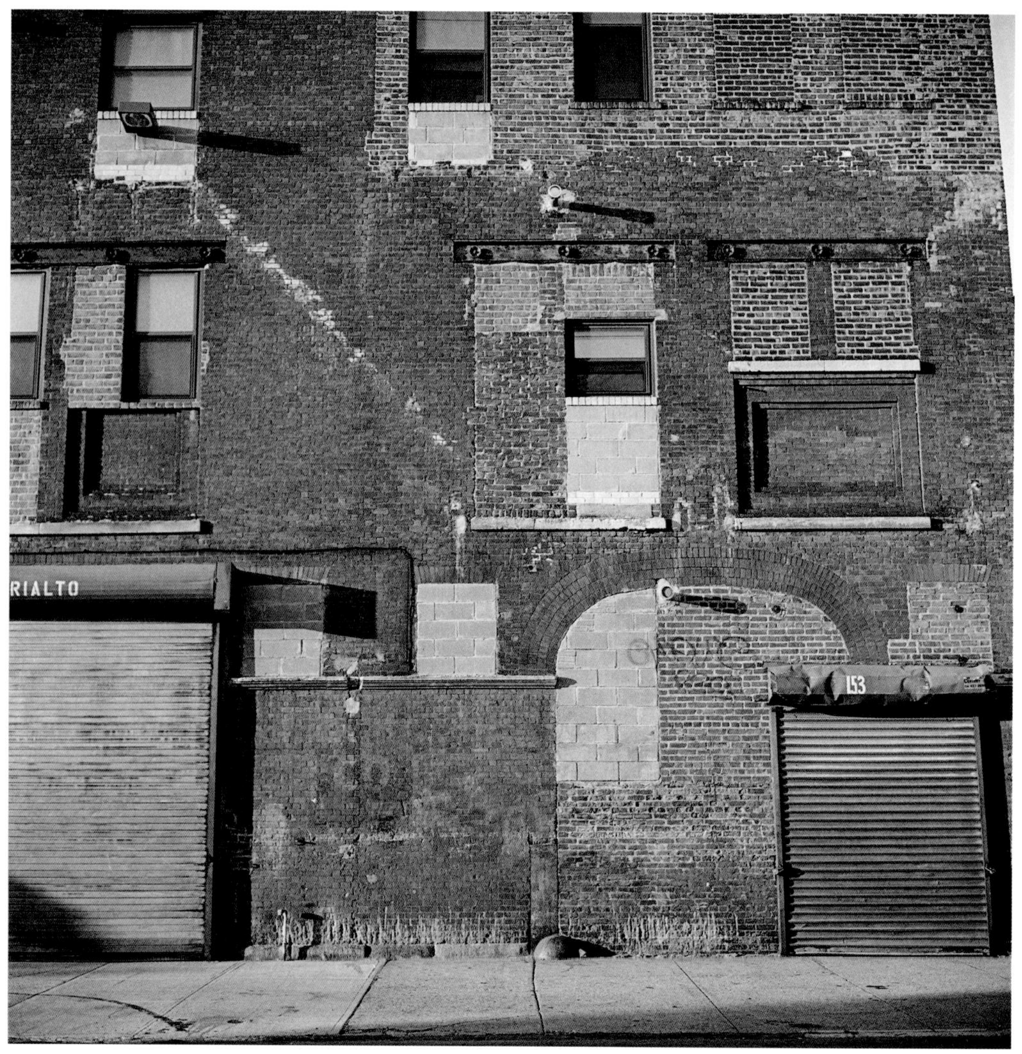
RIALTO
153

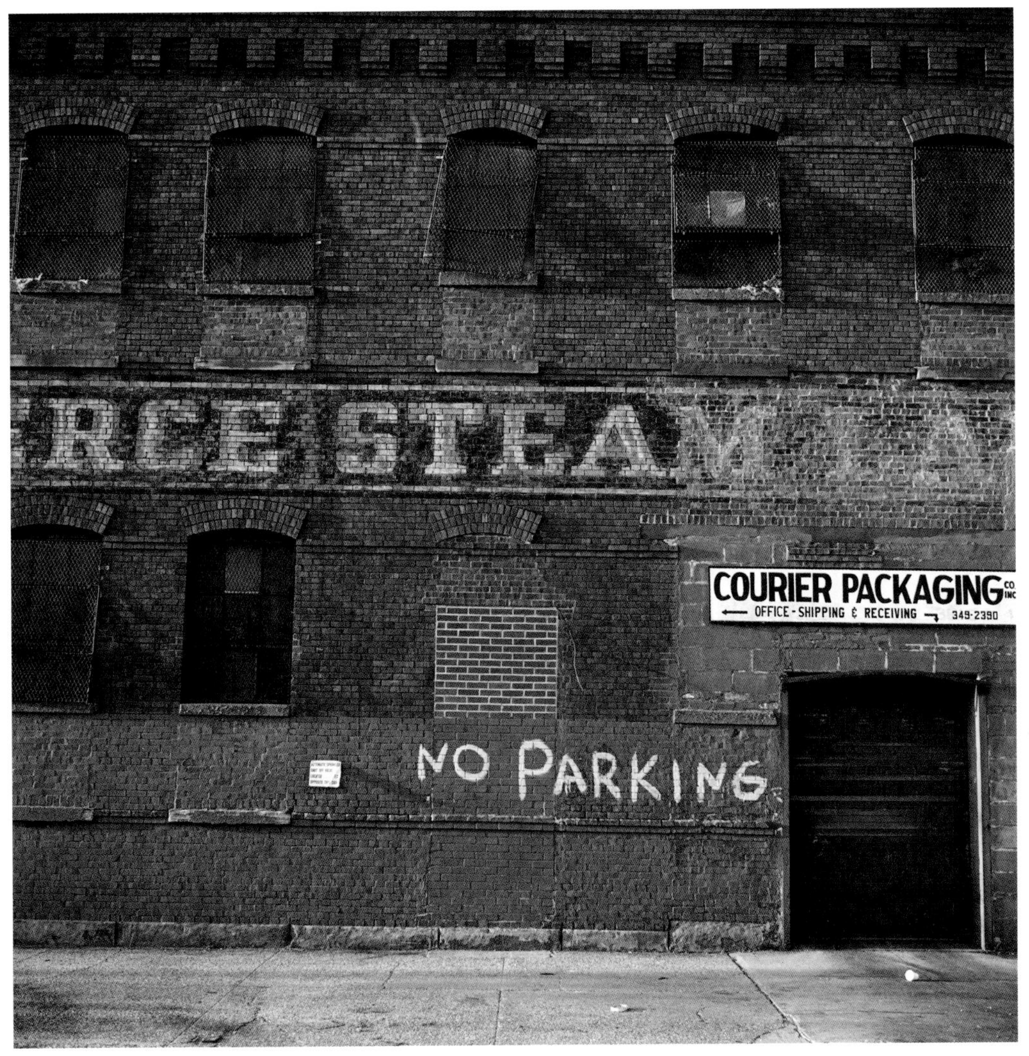
RCE STEA
COURIER PACKAGING
OFFICE - SHIPPING & RECEIVING
349-2390
NO PARKING

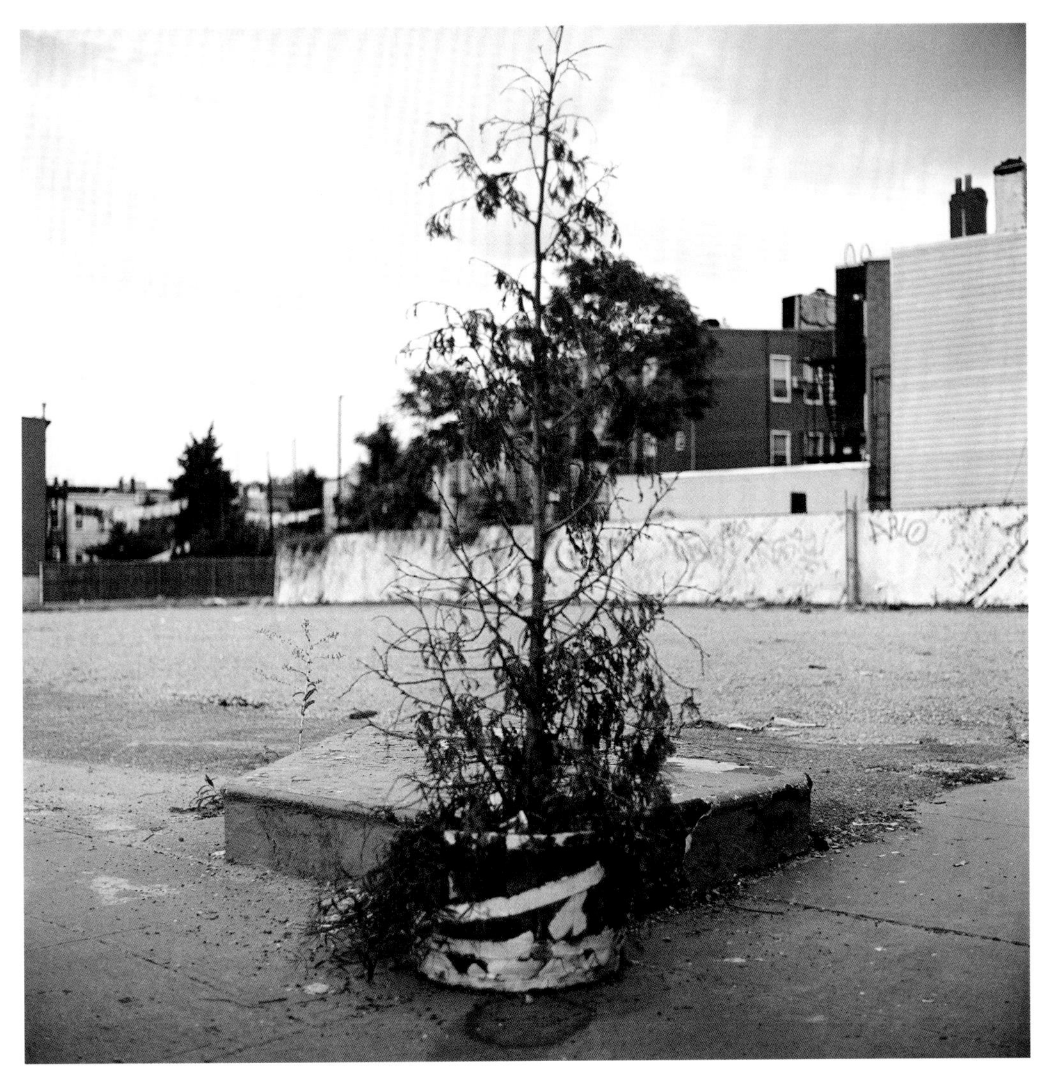

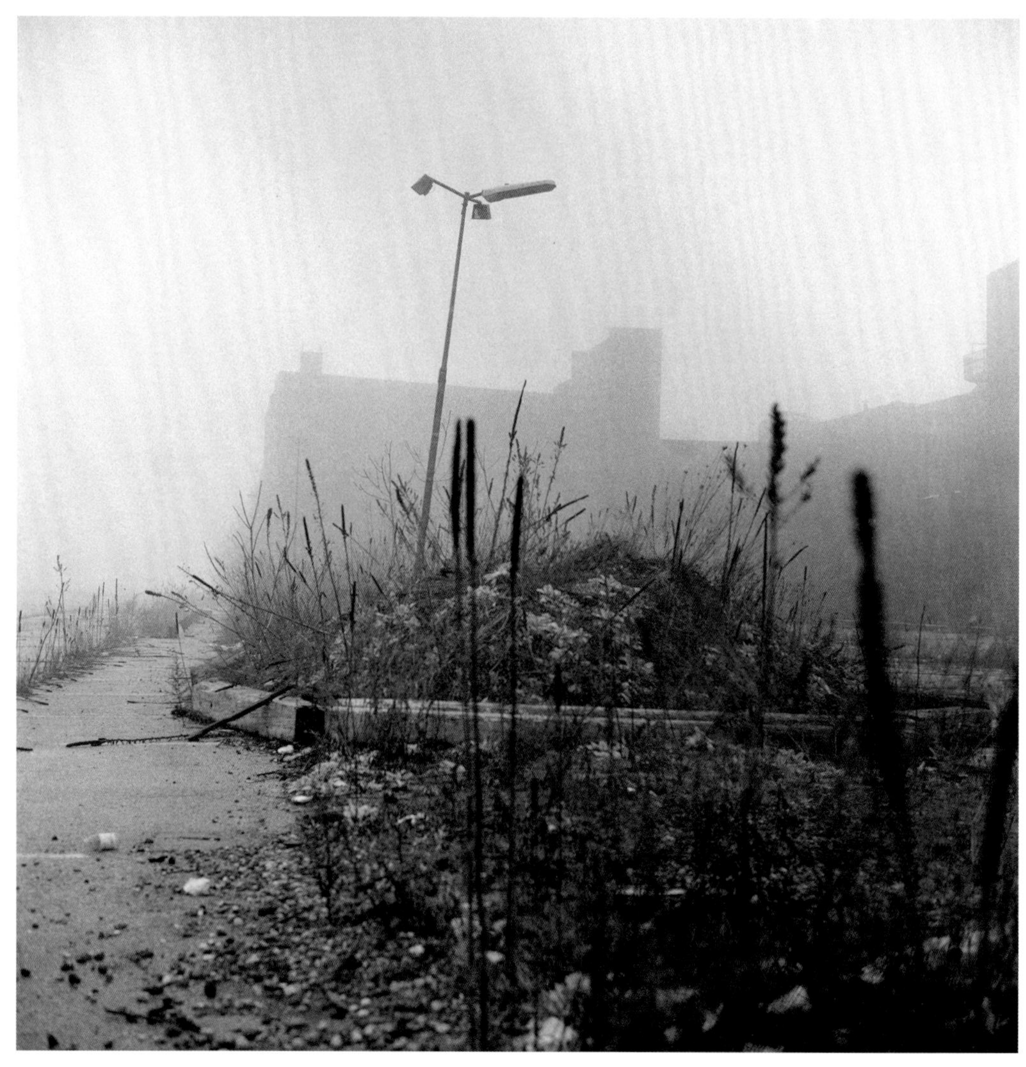

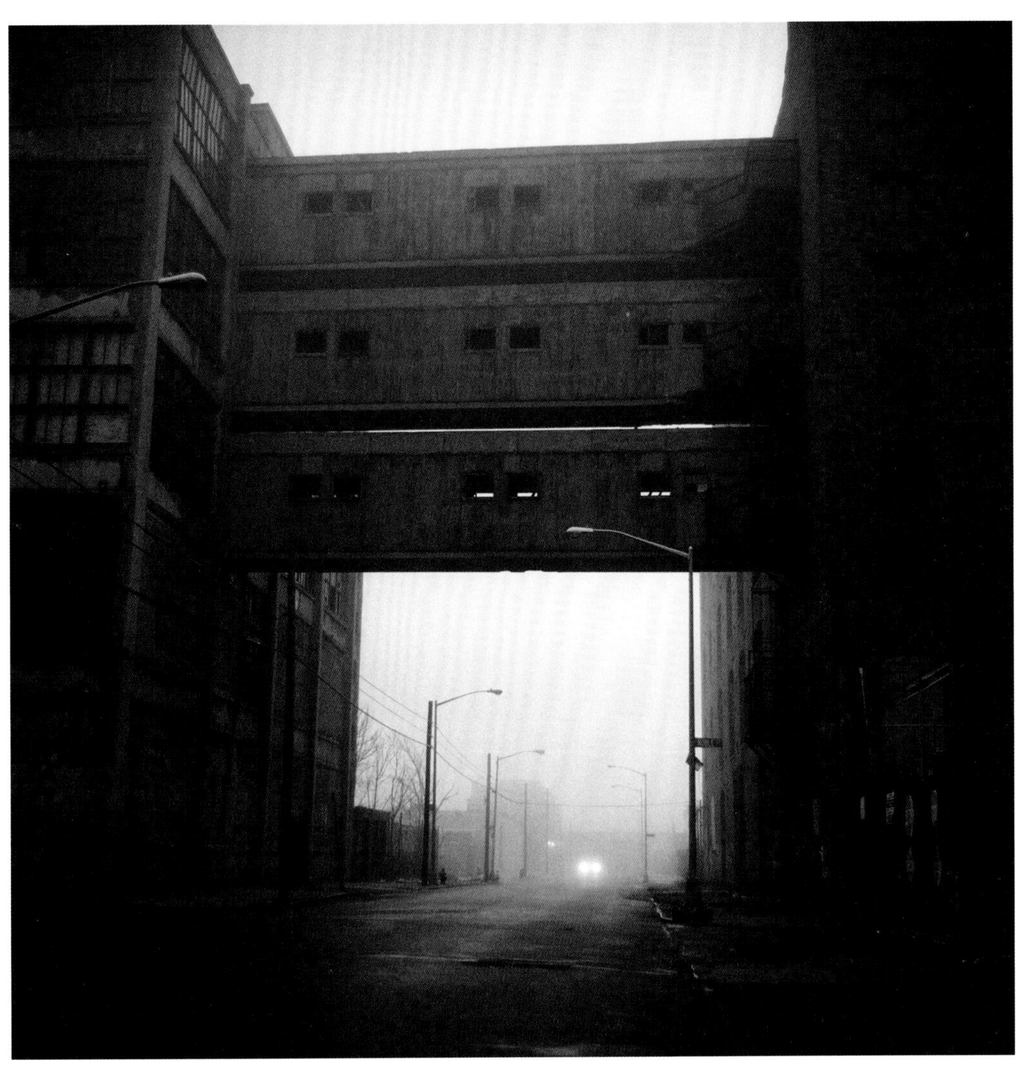

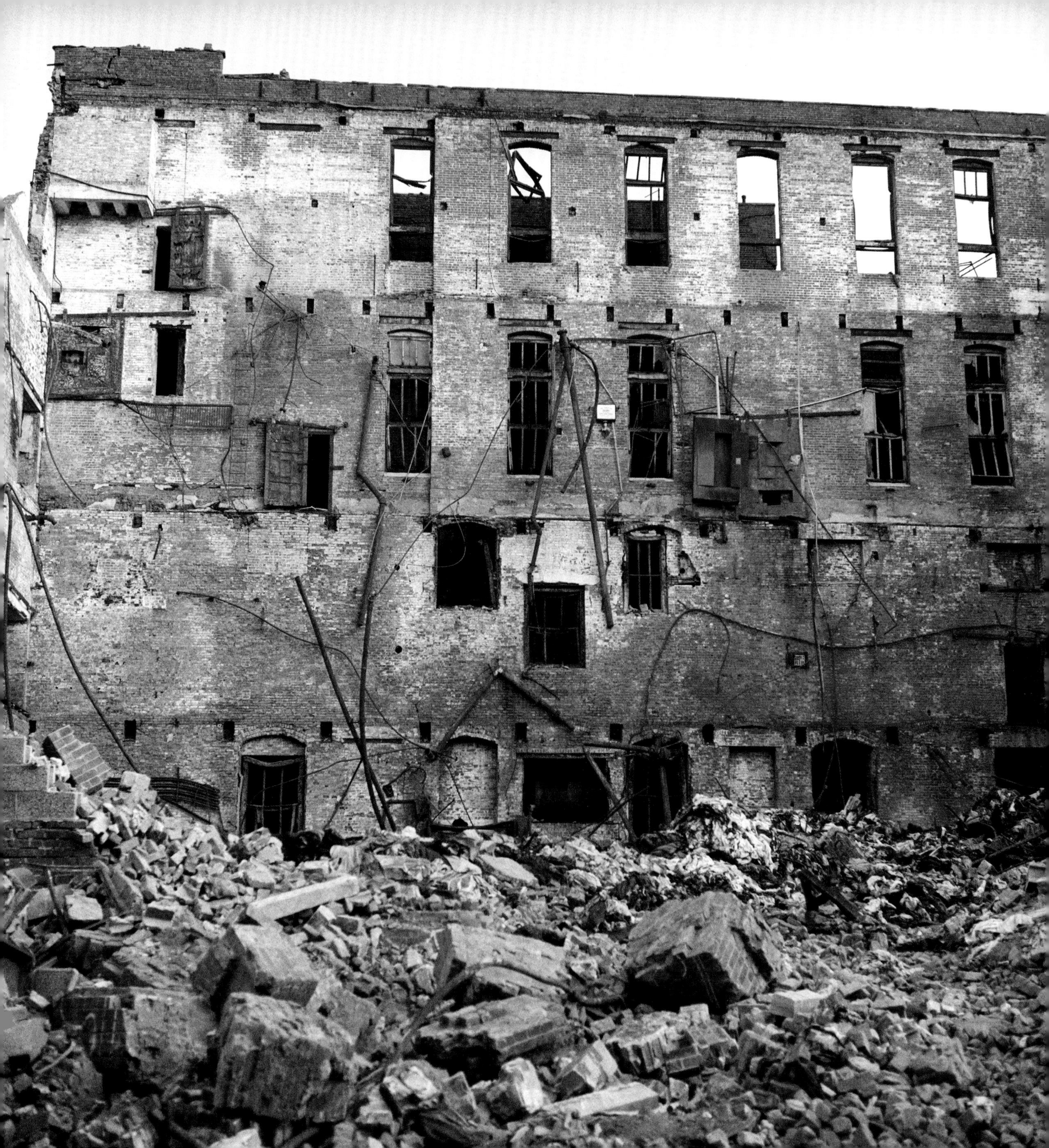

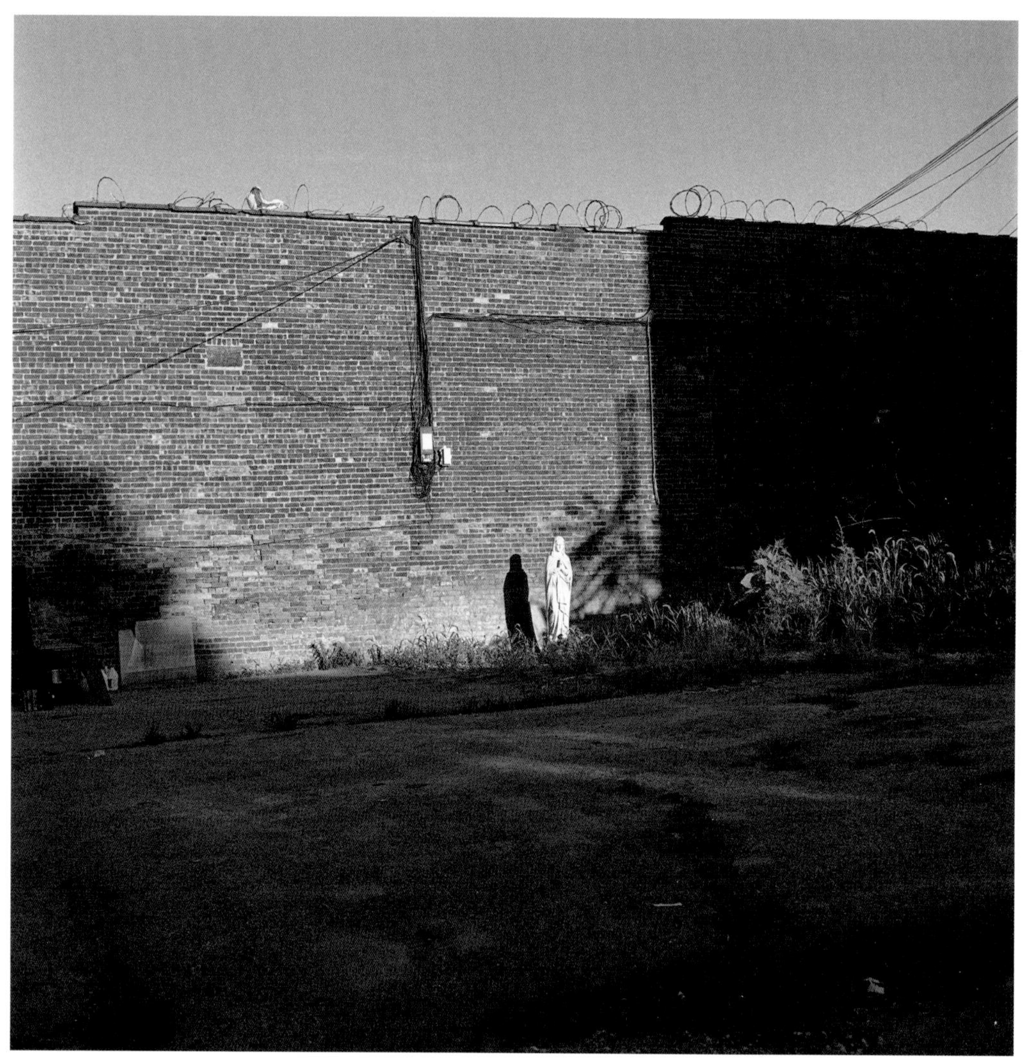

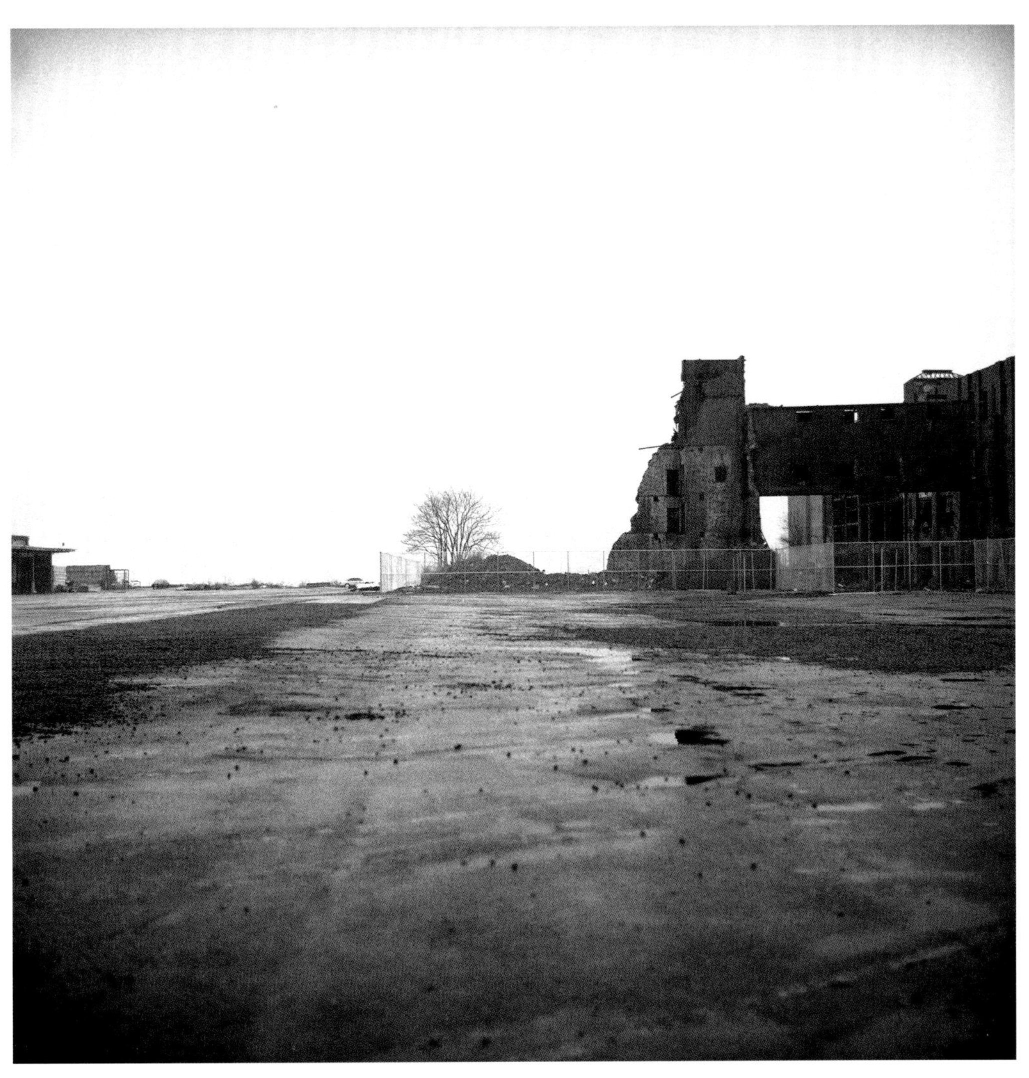

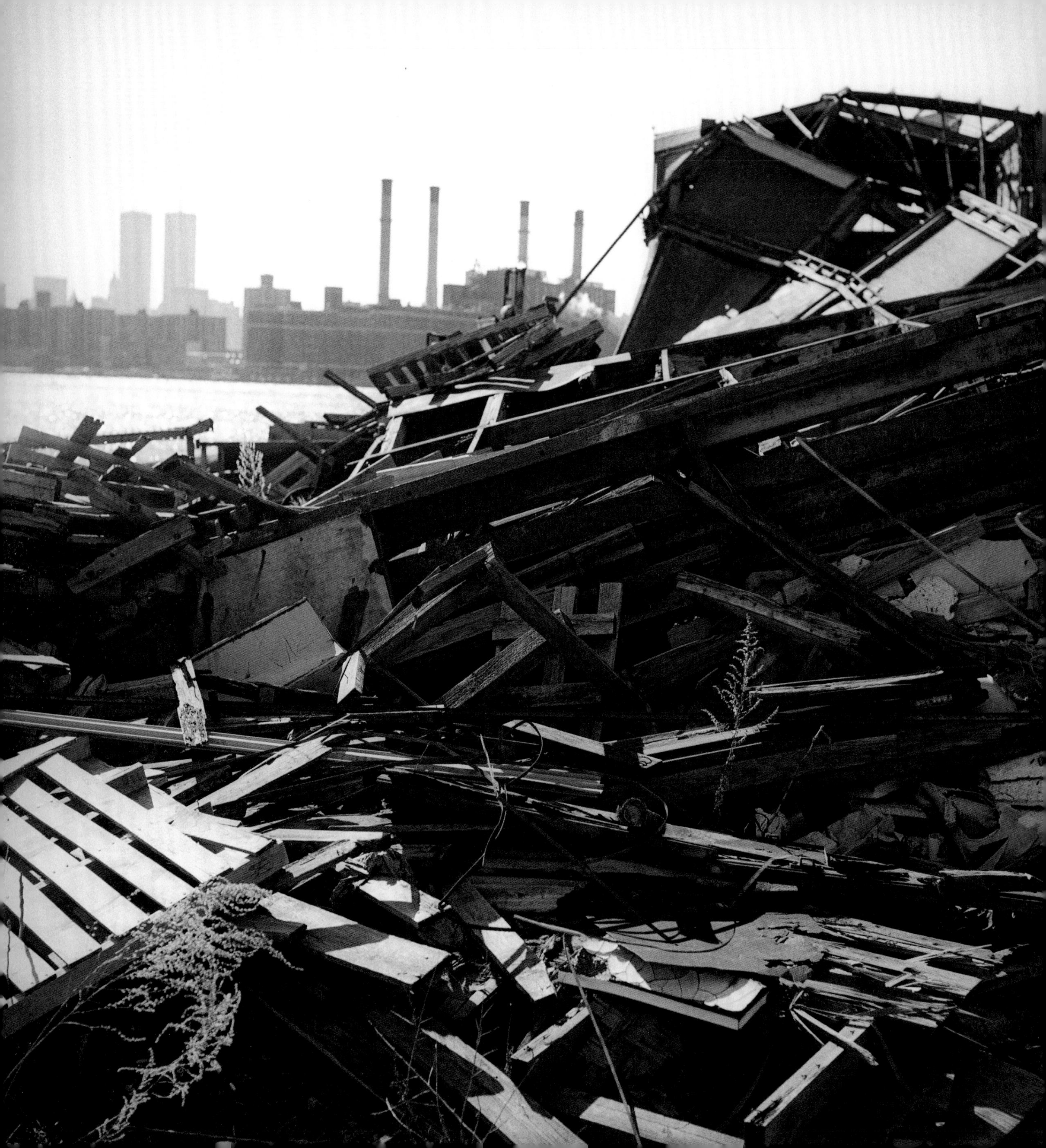

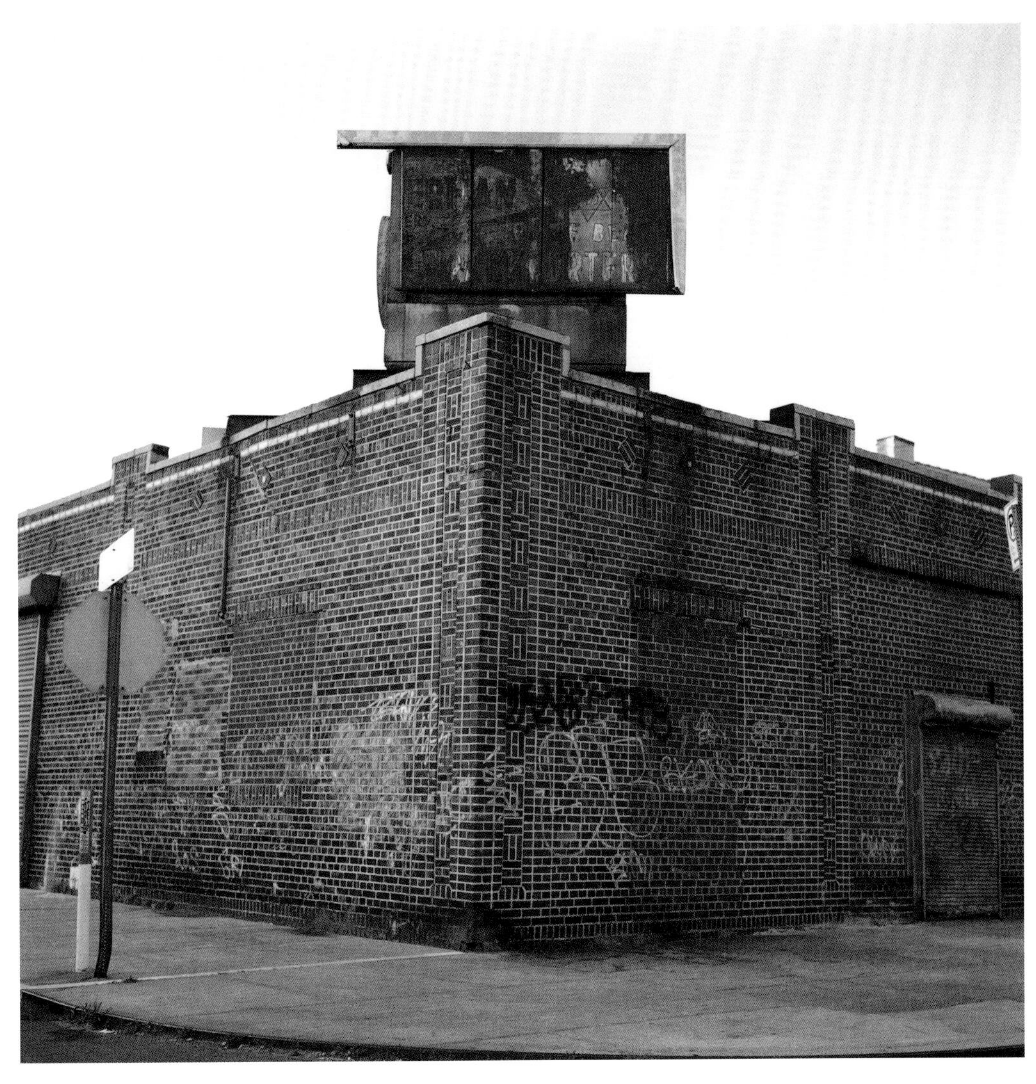

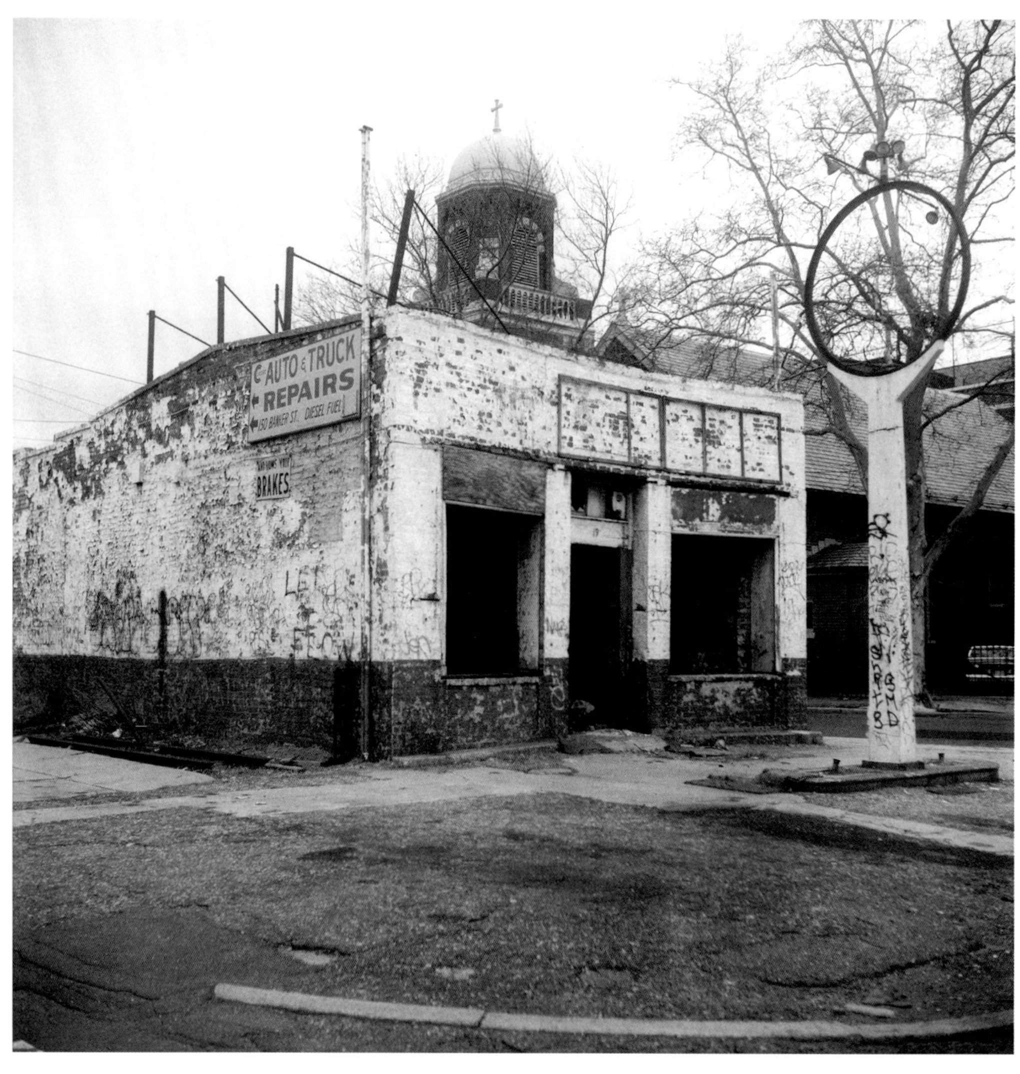
AUTO & TRUCK
REPAIRS
150 BAKER ST. DIESEL FUEL
BRAKES

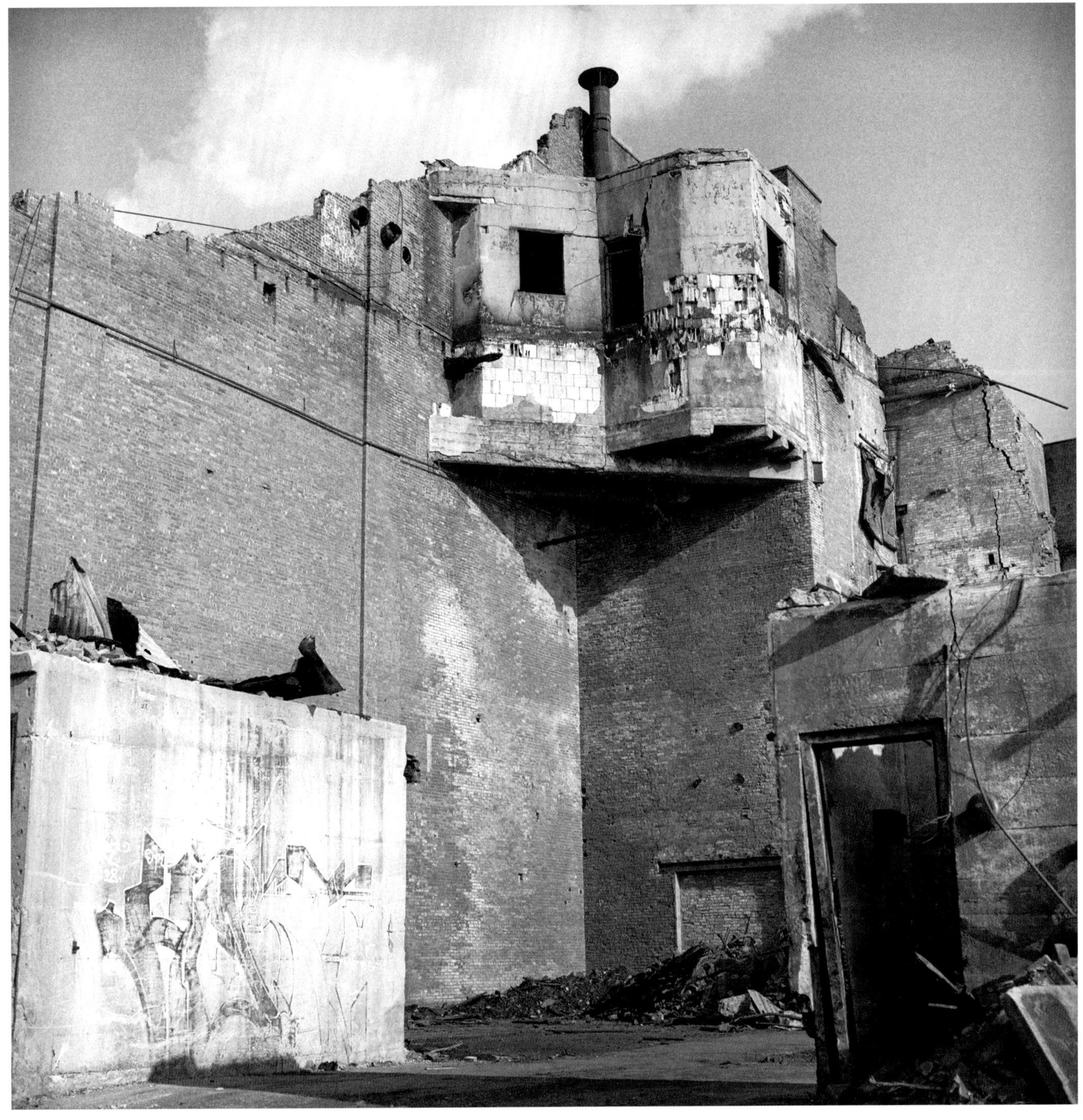

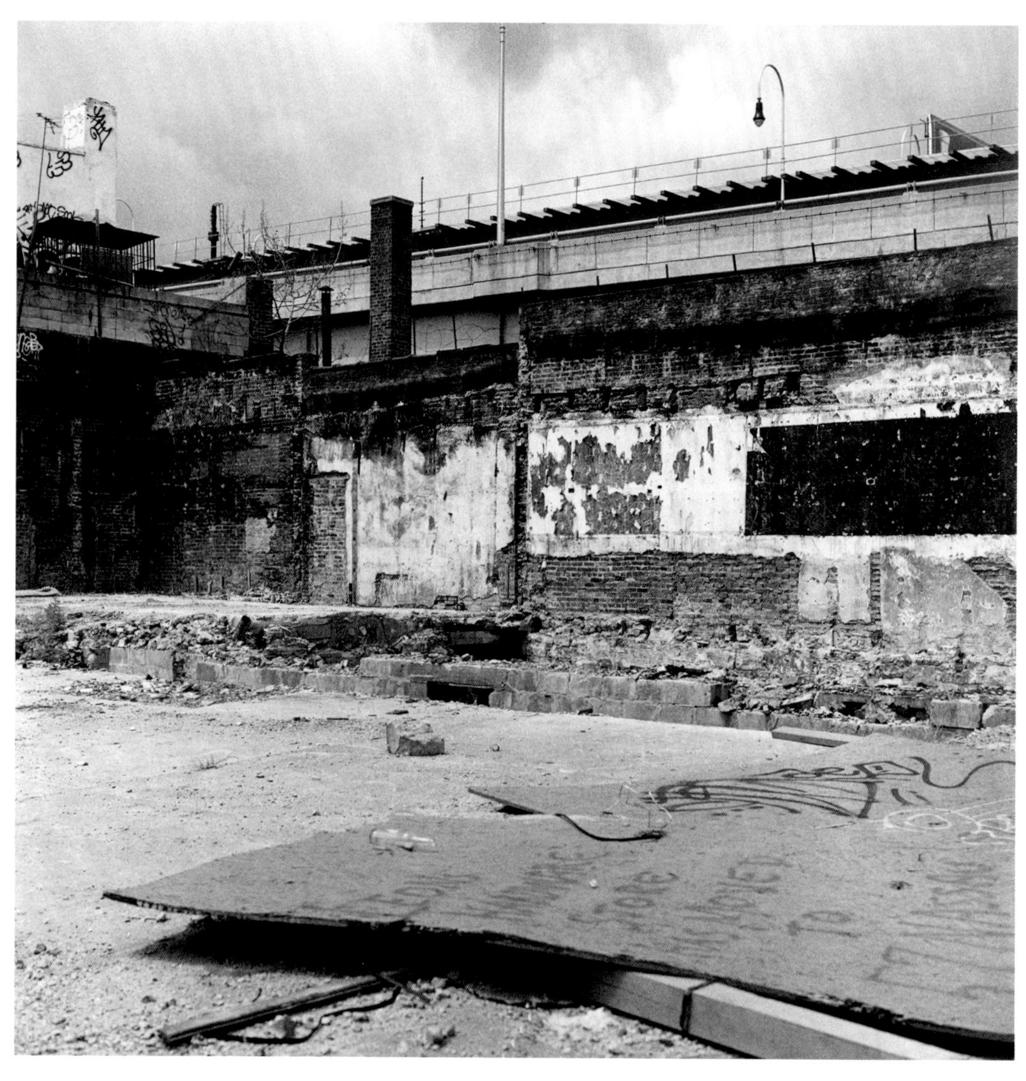

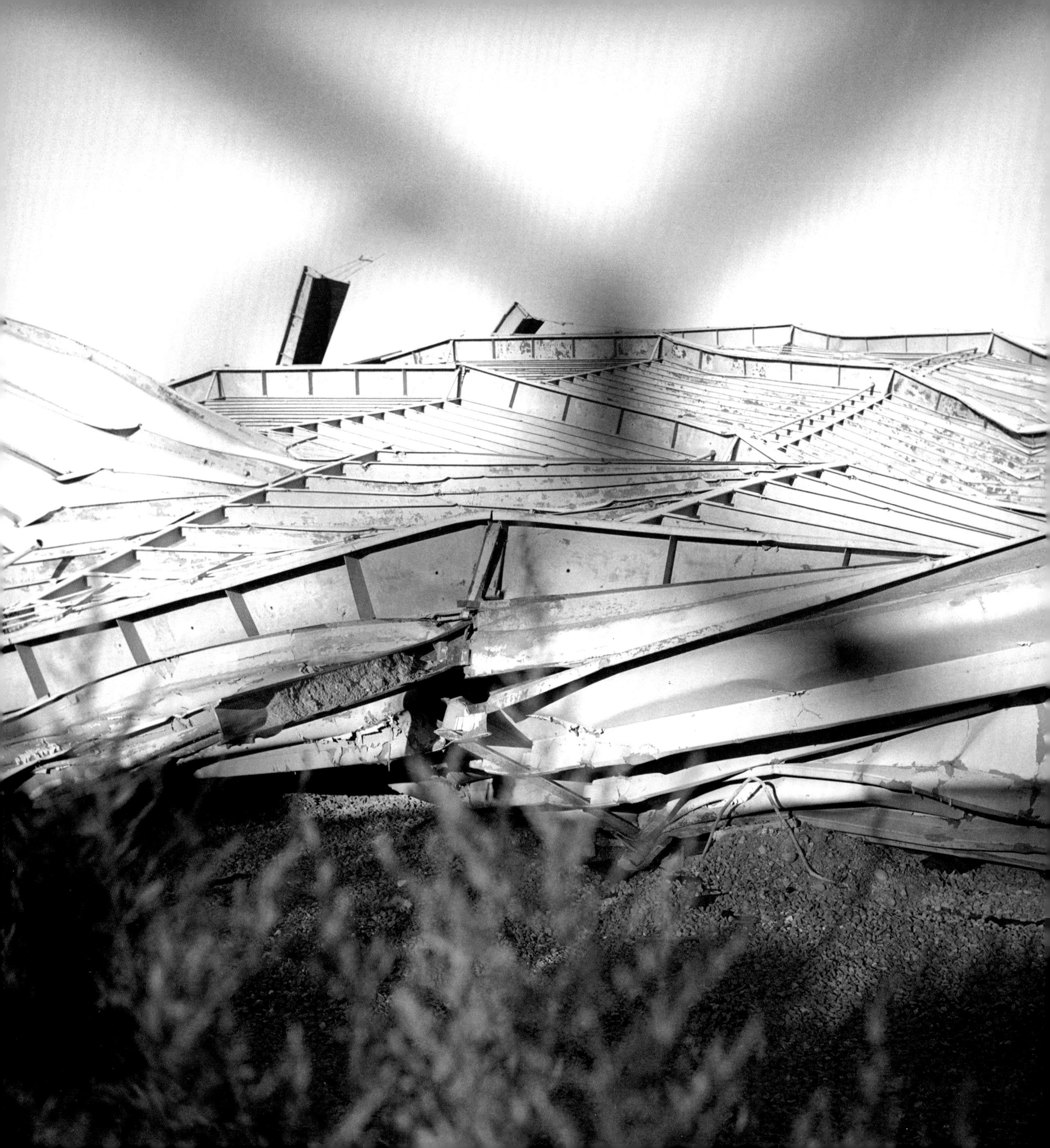

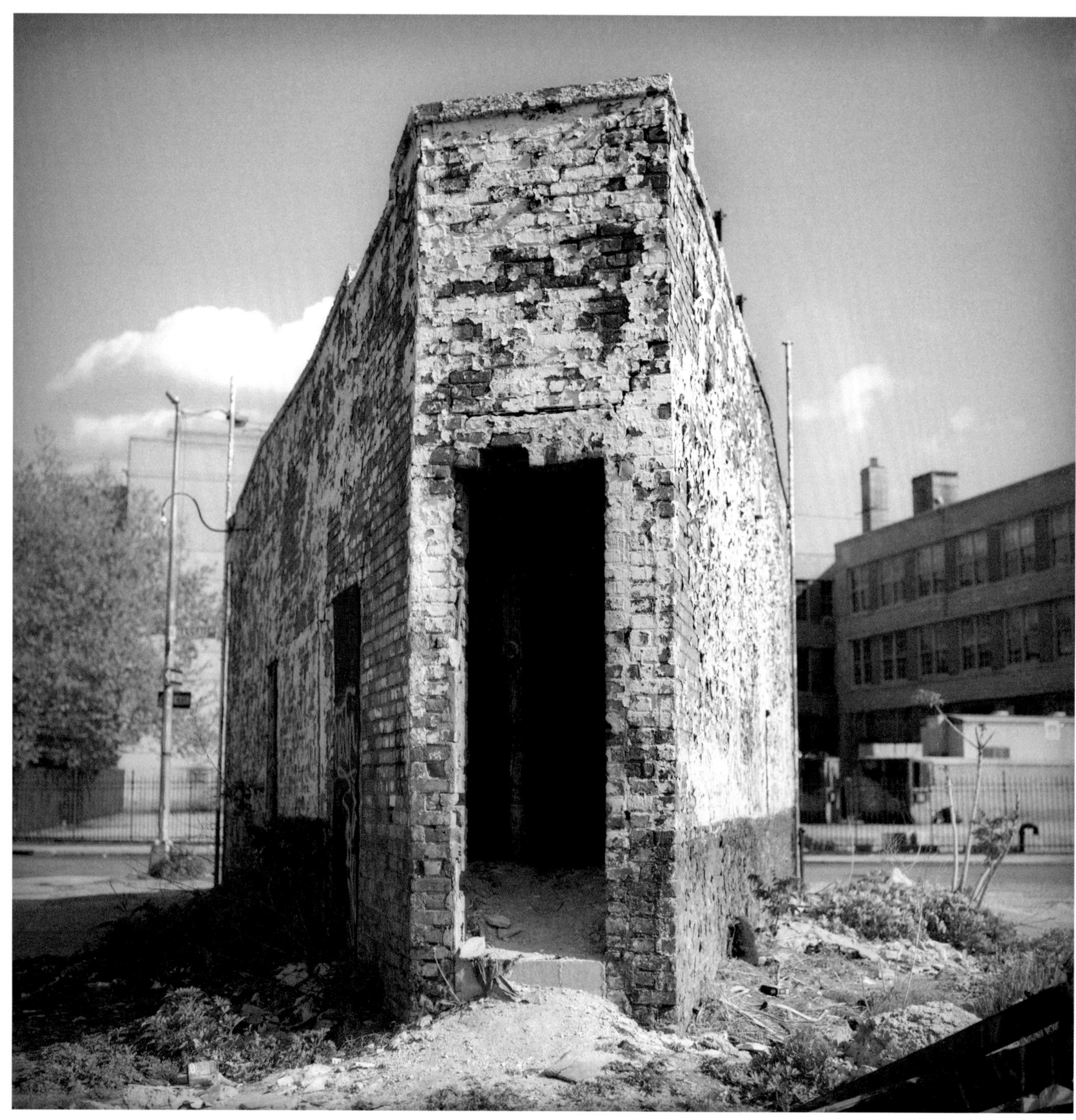